The Cambridge Manuals of Science and
Literature

METHODISM

T0345956

JOHN WESLEY

From the portrait in the National Gallery by Nathaniel Hone, R.A.

METHODISM

BY

H. B. WORKMAN, D.Lit.

Principal of the Westminster
Training College

Cambridge :
at the University Press

1912

CAMBRIDGE UNIVERSITY PRESS
Cambridge, New York, Melbourne, Madrid, Cape Town,
Singapore, São Paulo, Delhi, Tokyo, Mexico City

Cambridge University Press
The Edinburgh Building, Cambridge CB2 8RU, UK

Published in the United States of America by Cambridge University Press, New York

www.cambridge.org
Information on this title: www.cambridge.org/9781107626584

© Cambridge University Press 1912

First published 1912
First paperback edition 2011

A catalogue record for this publication is available from the British Library

ISBN 978-1-107-62658-4 Paperback

*With the exception of the coat of arms at
the foot, the design on the title page is a
reproduction of one used by the earliest known
Cambridge printer, John Siberch,* **1521**

PREFACE

In this short sketch of a great subject the author has tried to put himself into the critical but not unfriendly position of the interested outsider, for whom primarily this volume is intended. This is especially the case in Chapter IV. on the Divisions of Methodism, and in Chapter V. on the Theology and Polity of Methodism.

It will be perfectly obvious that, in so short a sketch as the present, many questions have had to be dealt with briefly, which in a work on a larger scale could have been more generously treated.

H. B. W.

March, 1912.

CONTENTS

METHODISM

CHAPTER I

THE EIGHTEENTH CENTURY

ARGUMENT

I

To the student of the history of the English-speaking races the story of Methodism must always form one of considerable interest. A Church which enfolds some thirty millions of adherents; which has established itself in every quarter of the globe,

A   1

with especial prominence in the United States;
which is to-day, with the possible exception of the
Lutheran Church, the largest Protestant Church
in the world, certainly the largest Church of the
English race, Protestant or otherwise; whose
indirect influence has been almost as great as its
direct—is manifestly a fact in the sphere of the
spiritual which cannot be ignored even by those
who would on *a priori* grounds refuse to recognise
its apostolic origin, or its ecclesiastical claims.
In these pages, leaving on one side all that is con-
troversial, the attempt will be made to set forth
in briefest compass the origins and meaning of
Methodism, with such facts in its later history
as may be of more general interest.

We have stated that Methodism, with its millions
of adherents in the United States, is the largest
Church of English races in the world. To the
English Anglican who has never travelled in America
or in the English Colonies, above all, to the Scot
familiar only with the predominant Presbyterianism
of his native country, such a statement will come,
perhaps, with surprise. Assuming the accuracy of
the claim, we may point out the close connection
there is between the vast extension of Methodism
in the modern world and the time of its origin.
For Methodism was the outcome of the eighteenth
century. Now it is the fashion in certain quarters

to look upon that century as lifeless. But it is in the eighteenth century, and in the movements, religious and political, of that most interesting age, that we discern the beginnings of the great currents, economic, social, political, intellectual, and religious, that govern the modern world. In the eighteenth century we see the older systems crumbling away under the dissolvent action of forces created and fed by the vanishing age. On all sides we note the signs of a fundamental reconstruction, culminating in Methodism and the French Revolution, in their diverse ways the most tremendous phenomena of the century, the first for the English-speaking races, the second for the world at large.

But Methodism would have been of but slight importance had not its origin coincided with the remarkable development and expansion in the political and social life of the English people. In the eighteenth century, the century that is which, properly, may be said to begin with the death of Anne and to close with the Congresses of Vienna (1714-1816), three features in the expansion of Great Britain stand out clear and distinct—the growth and consolidation of the empire and its colonies, including the United States ; the organisation of the Parliamentary State, and the beginning of democracy ; and the rise of the industrial revolution. Each of these great features in the evolution of the national life has contributed to the place and power of Methodism. But as the chief effect of the new democratic ideas was seen in the internal history of Methodism itself, we shall defer any consideration of this factor to a later chapter, and confine our attention for the present to the other two.

Of these three factors the first, the physical extension of the English race, is the simplest. In the sixteenth century, in her conflict with Spain, England first discovered the value of sea-power ; in the eighteenth century a series of fortunate events gave to her a hold upon the greater part of the undeveloped portions of the globe. For England the Seven Years' War was a turning-point in her national history, as indeed it was in the history of the world. England ceased to be a mere European power, whose position was determined by its place in a single continent ; henceforth she claimed the Empire of the Seas, and that her destinies lay in the lands beyond the oceans. The voyages and discoveries of Cook ; the intrepid adventures of North American trappers ; the irresistible impulse which drew the settlers westward over the Alleghanies to the blue grass of Kentucky, on " to the Father of the Waters," and the Rockies beyond ; the war which, by the fall of Quebec and the capture of Pittsburg and Louisburg, changed New France into the future Dominion of Canada ; the European struggles which led to the cession of the mighty area of Louisiana first to Spain, afterwards to the infant States ; the strange events which, in the next century, were destined to evolve a mighty continent from a penal settlement at Botany Bay ; the fortune which handed over an outpost of Dutch farmers and merchants at the Cape to the government of a country that, happily, knew not of the troubles the gift was destined to bring in its train—all these were part of the forces which gave to the revival, begun by the Wesleys, its world-wide opportunity. But for these Methodism could have become little more than a small sect of English Nonconformists—a position that still, by the ignorant, is so commonly assigned to her—instead of a vast imperial Church. One illustration of the importance of these factors must suffice. Let the reader take the map of North America as it was in 1712, and he will note a little strip of English settlers hemmed in on all sides by the dominions of France and Spain. If fortune had dealt otherwise in the conflicts at Pittsburg (1758), on the Heights of Abraham (1759), and in Acadia (1757), the opportunity of Methodism might have been as slight as it still is in the French provinces of Quebec, or in the Spanish countries beneath the Southern Cross.

In the marvellous expansion of the English-speaking race, of which the eighteenth century saw the beginnings, Methodism obtained her supreme advantage. No spiritual revival, however deep, could have produced the Methodist Church of to-day if it had found the ground already occupied, or if it had been retained, like some medieval order of monks or friars, within the parent Church. But when, whether from latent forces within herself or by the folly or apathy of the bishops, Methodism was driven out of the Anglican Church, she discovered on all sides vast opportunities, some the result of new circumstances, others the issue of neglect. A simple illustration from to-day will make our meaning clear. The early years of the twentieth century have witnessed the great marvel of the re-awakening of the East. A chance has arisen the like of which has never been seen in missionary annals since the fall of the Roman Empire. As yet none can say what section of the one Church will respond to the call and claim for her Master the heritage of the East. To-day, as in the third century, the future of the world, it may be the future of the Church of Christ, lies with the denomination that seizes aright the great missionary opportunities of the age. In the seventh and eighth centuries the Roman Church established herself by the response she gave, under the lead of Gregory the Great, to the call of the barbarians, Saxons,

Danes, and the like. In the twentieth century the church or denomination that rises to the need of China or Japan or India—be she Protestant or Roman—will be the Church of the future, in spite of all *a priori* reasonings or prepossessions. Hers will be the logic of established fact. So in the eighteenth century we witness a similar crisis, a similar opportunity, though limited, broadly speaking, to the Anglo-Saxon race. The annexation by the English of the uninhabited portions of the world was not the less the great fact of the century because it was so largely undesigned, we might almost write, accidental. In an empire founded by design provision would have been made for the transference to the new provinces of the established religion of the centre. As a matter of fact, such provision was almost totally ignored, as we see from the constant refusal of the English Government to allow the ordination of bishops for America. The failure of the Anglican Church, for reasons partly political partly spiritual, to respond to the needs of the expanding Empire issued in Methodism stepping in her own way into the vacant place, and thereby securing the remarkable position that she now holds.

II

If to the expansion of Britain we owe the world-
wide extension of Methodism, its hold at home
must be largely traced to the industrial revolution
of the century. At the birth of Wesley the most
populous counties, next to Surrey and Middlesex,
were Somerset, Wilts, Oxford, Suffolk, and other
country districts, none of which, however, had on
the average more than sixty individuals to the
square mile. At the commencement of the eight-
teenth century, England and Wales had a population
considerably less than that of modern London, for
the most part rural in character and pursuits, or
living under the shadow of some ancient cathedral,
or in some small county town whose picturesque
decay to-day tells us of a vanished age. Apart
from the capital, Bristol, Norwich and York were
the only cities of any size, while the population
of Worcestershire was more dense than that of
Lancashire or Yorkshire. But within the lifetime
of Wesley all this was changed. By the year 1800
England had become the workshop of the world,
at that time the sole industrial State in existence.
She had ceased to be the nation of shopkeepers
that Louis XIV. had called her, not without some
justification, and had become a nation of artisans
and capitalists. The result of this industrial growth

of the latter part of the eighteenth century was a revolution in which the older England, the England which for a thousand years had developed slowly but continuously on certain definite lines, passed away for ever. A new England was born, at first misshapen, undesirable, unconscious of herself ; nor were there absent the usual pangs and pains of an unexpected birth.

With the incoming of the age of iron and steam, the centre of gravity was shifted from the rural south to the new populations north of the Humber. On all sides we see the influx from the country into the towns, the depopulation of the country ; this last aided by the selfish system of enclosures—the great legalised crime of the age—which deprived the villagers, without compensation, of the rights in the soil that for centuries had been theirs.   But the towns, for the most part, were not the old boroughs. London, it is true, maintained its pre-eminence, and Bristol struggled, though ineffectually, to adapt its trade to the new conditions.   But Manchester, Liverpool, Glasgow, Birmingham, Sheffield, Leeds and Bradford were almost the new creations of the industrial revolution, and of a commerce that more and more turned its gaze away from Europe and the old trade-routes towards the West.   Vast as were the growths of population in the towns in the nineteenth century, they but accentuated the results already accomplished by the industrial revolution in the last thirty years of the eighteenth century. The England of to-day, so far at any rate as its organised life is concerned, is essentially the development of the England of 1780 ; separated from the England of 1680 by a gulf almost as deep and broad as that which divides the England of Charles II. from medieval times.

For the shifting of population from country to town was the least important element in the new England. The inhabitants of the new towns soon showed characteristics, the product of their toil and of their specialised skill, that cut them off from the slow-going, conservative dwellers round some cathedral close or in the southern villages. In many directions we see the cracking and crumbling of the old social and economic structure. Territorial feudalism gave place to the new relations of capital and labour. The new towns, with their teeming life, found the old ideals impossible, and demanded new creeds, new economics, new politics and a new literature. On all sides we see the rise of new problems—the drink question, the need of popular education, and of a reform of the Poor Law, are three instances out of many that will occur to the thoughtful—the result of the new, ill-regulated, unorganised industrialism.

Unhappily for herself, in this hour of revolution,

the Church of England was almost wholly unable to adapt herself to the new needs. Her parochial system had become stereotyped by the centuries. Where a thousand new churches and schools would have been none too many, she built with niggard hand but here and there. Under Walpole's administration a full stop was even put to Queen Anne's scheme for the building of fifty-two additional churches in London. The Anglican clergy were, for the most part, country Tories, cut off, through the necessities of the Hanoverian dynasty, from all influence upon government ; fatally cut off, by education and politics, from either understanding of, or sympathy with, the new populations. Her bishops, who should have been the first to see the needs of the hour, were largely court Whigs, nominees of the Crown, through their politics thus cut off from their clergy, over whom they kept the political watch, which to some of their number appeared the whole duty of spiritual overseers. Even if they had been accepted as leaders they had few of the qualities which would have guided the Anglican Church in the new problems which confronted her. Where the economic and social dislocation of the age demanded a constructive statesmanship instinct with love, the bishops, with rare exceptions, showed that they were unaware of any problem that needed attention. Where the people, in their inarticulate misery, cried out for bread, they gave them a stone ; instead of the living water they supplied them with rivers of ink ; in place of leadership through the wilderness they advocated a stern repression. So once again, at home as in the Colonies, the English Church lost her opportunity. When, after the Oxford Movement, she awoke to the call, she found that the new populations had largely fallen away from her to the older Dissenters and the new Methodists. These, at any rate, however imperfectly, had tried to understand their needs. But in Scotland the new industrialism which turned Glasgow from a small town sheltering beneath its cathedral into a mighty metropolis, found a native Presbyterianism alive to its wants—at any rate possessing the latent qualities needed—and so rejected the Methodism which appealed to the southrons.

III

In her inelasticity of methods, in her blindness to the great needs of the day, the Church of England was only too truly representative of the nation at large, and of the statesmen who lost the American colonies because of their inability to discern the signs of the times. To the student of the eighteenth century nothing is more remarkable than the intensity with which the eighteenth century interested itself in what are now seen to have been the merest trifles, the blindness it displayed to the great elemental forces working below the surface. Its history, until stung from unconsciousness into reality by the great fact of the French Revolution, too often disgusts by the pettiness of its political cabals and the grossness of its financial abuses, by the brutality of its legal system, and by the insufferable arrogance with which a landed class, wrapped up in its pleasures, resisted or mutilated, when it could not reject, every movement towards reform. Yet a keener vision discerns beneath the mass of corruption and intrigue the slow transference of executive authority from the Crown to the Cabinet, the slow rise of the new democracy. We remember that in spite of politicians it was in the eighteenth century that we won India, and, by the capture of Quebec, determined the future of America. The more we look back the more we are amazed at the apparent accidents which in the eighteenth century gave us a world-wide empire, of the extent and future of which the shrewdest thinkers had neither dreams nor visions. To-day we see clearly the great results hidden from the eyes of the age that wrought them. Trivial as were oftentimes the ostensible causes of her constant wars—the war of Jenkins' ear may serve as an

example—we now know that upon them depended
the most tremendous issues. As usual, unknown
to ourselves, we blundered into success. The
battles fought in Flanders, or beyond the
Rhine, to bring the Bourbons to their knees, were
fought there in name alone. Their effect was to
open up the Great Lakes of Canada, to hand over to
us the great hinterland beyond the Alleghanies,
or to turn our trading factories in Bengal or on the
Coromandel coast into the beginnings of our Indian
Empire.

Equally remarkable was this blindness both in
the world of ideas and of social life. Absence of
foresight was the great characteristic of the age ;
the natural result of its constant policy — *tranquilla
non movere*. Through want of foresight, of power
to discern the new needs of a new world, Europe,
England included, lost its colonies, where a greater
sympathy, big ideas of adaptation and reconstruction, would have saved them. The unexpectedness
with which the French Revolution burst upon the
world is one of the commonplaces of history. In
English political life the same blindness was seen
in the dreary Toryism characteristic of the period,
which resisted all change simply because it was
change, and conceived that the one end of statesmanship was the defence of the rights of property
to the neglect of its duties, or the maintenance of

the existing social order by a ruthless regime of coercion and repression. Not less remarkable, however, was the blindness of our rulers to the meaning of the great forces, economical, social, and religious, which were slowly springing into being beneath the surface. And because these things were hidden from its eyes, the eighteenth century concerned itself with the superficial facts of a life whose picturesque, elegant charm has so fascinated all that we sometimes forget that the eighteenth century will be for ever memorable, not because of its beaux, its wits, its exquisite manners, its delightful dilettanteism, but because of the revolutionary forces that, unknown to itself, were maturing within its womb.

In the blindness and inelasticity of the Anglican Church in the eighteenth century, we find both the occasion and the opportunity of Methodism. But blindness and inelasticity, though sins unto death, are themselves the result of a deeper cause. Nothing is easier than to dwell on the worldliness of the Church of England in the eighteenth century. The historians of Methodism, as a rule, have made too much of the sins, the follies, the religious indifference, the open infidelity, the cultured licence, the grossness of life, the absence of any ideal of duty or spiritual sense which characterised the age, and had eaten out the life of the Church. The facts,

too familiar to need repetition, were sad enough
in all conscience. Even if the Church had been
alive she would have needed all her reserves of
strength in facing the vast problems of a new age.
As it was she had a name to live but was dead. At
the commencement of the century she had political
power in abundance, as we see from the Sacheverell
struggle, and from her passing such disgraceful
measures as the Occasional Conformity Act and the
Schism Act (1714). But such power is of no avail
where there is the absence of spiritual life ; in fact,
by its prostitution to selfish or intolerant ends,
such power becomes in the long run a positive
hindrance.

The reader should grasp clearly wherein the
weakness of the Anglican Church consisted. First
and foremost we put the absence of all spiritual
message. Even the nobler men in the Church, its
Seckers and Butlers, seem to have been unconscious
of any higher source of inspiration than reasonableness and moderation. In this absence of spiritual
vision the Church of England proved herself on the
same low level as the age before which she should
have upheld the ideals of the Cross. The century
was, in reality, in its early years especially, an age
of spiritual fatigue, of dim ideals and expiring hopes.
Instead of the great religious and political ideas of
the seventeenth century we have the age of Walpole

and the Pelhams, an age in which idealism and
self-sacrifice, with one or two great exceptions, are
conspicuous by their absence. The forces which
had produced the religious struggles of the previous
century had become exhausted, and had given place,
partly by reaction, to a hard uninspiring materialism,
opportunist in its methods, destitute of all the
nobler and more ideal elements of life, and, in
consequence, fatally degraded in its standards of
religion and ethics. On all sides the age was one
of inertia, of the absence of " visions," and of consequent spiritual sterility. As is usually the case
in a materialistic age we note the rapid disappearance
of doctrinal teaching, and the conversion of Christianity into a mere system of morality. The natural
results followed. The substitution of a moral for
the supernatural basis of religion led to the decay
of morality itself. The Church prided itself upon
its elimination of " enthusiasm," and upon its
practical tendencies ; the real result was extraordinary coarseness and inefficiency in all depart-
ments of life.

The effects of this national decadence are seen
in their most exaggerated forms in such hideous
scandals as the South Sea Bubble, and the passion
for gambling which seized the upper classes. More
lasting in its results was the extraordinary increase
of drinking, especially of gin, among all classes of

B

the community, and the rapid growth of all forms of lawlessness and crime. English philosophy, poetry, and religion were all alike dominated by the same lifeless materialism. In the sphere of thought this called itself rationalism. In the sphere of religion it resolved itself into a self-complacency unconscious of the fact of sin, and, therefore, of the need of a Saviour, that masqueraded as theoretical Deism, or as a benevolent neutrality between rival religions. Even poetry, under its influence, became so intensely didactic as to lose all its lyrical and natural notes. Turn where we will we see all upward longing lost in a destructive materialistic satisfaction with a level of effort or attainment that at the best was but decent mediocrity.

One special feature of this absence of spiritual message should be noted. In the reaction of the Restoration the Church had become so thoroughly Erastian that the leading tenet of her Christianity— if we may judge from the dying profession of Lake, Bishop of Chichester, from the national enthusiasm it evoked at the trial of Sacheverell (1710), from printed sermons innumerable, and from legal statutes, oaths of allegiance, and the like—would appear to have been the doctrine of non-resistance to the Divine Right of Kings. As Lecky has pointed out, "It occupied a more prominent place than any other tenet in the whole compass of theology."

The discredit of this doctrine, begun by the Revolution of 1688 and completed by the Hanoverian succession, was bound to react upon the influence of the Church which had proclaimed it as a cardinal tenet ; the more so, because, unfortunately for herself, the Church had nothing to take its place. With the accession of the Georges Erastianism merely took a new form. The Hanoverian statesman, Walpole, in especial, systematically degraded the Church into a useful state-engine. For this purpose, after silencing convocation, they governed a hostile Tory clergy by Whig bishops, selected for political, at best for intellectual rather than spiritual, considerations, whose latitudinarian doctrines, however much might have been said for them otherwise, were bitterly resented by High Church orthodoxy.

Such evidence as the Church showed of religious vitality was almost confined to the production of endless theological polemics, for the most part of the earth earthy and barren. Apologetics were poured out for Christianity, a few no doubt of permanent value, as all work must be which places Christianity upon a firm intellectual basis. But the greatest apology, the Christian life itself, was too conspicuously absent. The apologists, moreover, forgot that Christianity, if true to its genius and history, should always be on the attack against the gates of hell rather than sheltering behind the walls of syllogisms.

Even Butler's Analogy, with all its force of argument,
is the exhibition of Christianity upon its last line of
defence, as indeed to Butler's pessimistic mind it
would appear to have been. Not with such a theory
of Probabilism did the Church win its ancient
conquests. At all events the zeal for orthodoxy
of the few can never atone for the apathy in the
discharge of spiritual duties of the many. In the
case of the better placed clergy, including even
such men as Butler, absenteism was the rule rather
than the exception. In ten parishes round Cheddar
there was not a single resident curate. The devotion
of such men as Walker of Truro, Fletcher of Madeley,
Grimshaw of Haworth, Berridge of Everton, and
William Romaine, could not make up for the general
indifference of the parochial clergy and the utter
lack of organisation. Owing largely to the pluralities
whereby the few were gorged at the expense of the
many, the parish clergy, for the most part, were
ill-paid, of low social position, oftimes cringing
and obsequious. Unfortunately also some of the
saintliest of the clergy were non-Jurors, *e.g.* Jeremy
Collier and William Law, who were thus cut off
from their due influence. Though in the large
towns the clergy as a whole were of superior stamp,
they had little spiritual influence with their congregations, and, for that matter, in too many cases
showed little desire to possess it. When Romaine

filled St George's, Hanover Square, with " a ragged, unsavoury multitude " attracted by his preaching, his vicar was the first to forbid him the pulpit.

Nevertheless, though the facts of spiritual decadence are beyond dispute, we must beware of exaggeration. Historians, we think, have sometimes attached too much weight to the well-known utterances of Butler, they have forgotten the pessimism so habitual with him that he declined the archbishopric of Canterbury on the ground that it was " too late for him to try to support a falling Church." We are in some danger, in dealing with the eighteenth century, of being misled by its writers and politicians, and of forgetting the great middle and lower middle classes—never more inarticulate than in that age of surface-culture.

The need of avoiding exaggeration, so far as the middle classes are concerned, is especially seen when we consider the number and extent of the religious societies, composed almost without exception of members of the Anglican Church, which to some extent anticipated the society classes of Wesley. The formation of these can be dated back as far as 1678, and during the first thirty years of the century they flourished exceedingly, largely through the influence of William Law's *Serious Call to a Devout and Holy Life*. The intention of one and all was " to quicken each other's affection towards spiritual things." But from seeking to save their own souls they soon passed by the inevitable transition into the attempt to save the souls of others ; as Law puts it, " that some might be relieved by their charities, and all be blessed with their prayers, and benefited by their example." Unfortunately, though hedged about with precautions to keep them within Church lines, they became the object of suspicion to the dignitaries of the Church, who, at the first show of " enthusiasm " or earnestness, showed an hostility which eventually ruined them.

The existence of these Anglican societies is, however, but a detail. There are larger grounds for bewaring of exaggeration. The political defeat of Puritanism has led many writers to overlook the degree to which it had woven new strands of abiding influence into the life of the nation. The surface-facts of the eighteenth century must not mislead us. Beneath all the froth and scum that floated on the top the waters of the river of life still ran deep though not always clear. We see this in the lives of such laymen as Samuel Johnson and Edmund Burke, of the Countess of Huntingdon and Lady Elizabeth Hastings, and of such bishops as the saintly Thomas Wilson of Sodor and Man. George I. may have been a murderer, as Lord Acton claimed, a murderer " whose proper destination should have been not St James' but Newgate, and indeed not

Newgate but Tyburn "; Frederick, Prince of Wales, was probably, to quote his own mother's verdict, " the greatest ass, and the greatest liar, and the greatest *canaille*, and the greatest beast in the whole world " ; an utter lack of decorum and morality alike may have characterised Walpole and his circle ; but, after all, English home life in the main was still pure in spite of its corrupt court and aristocracy. Voltaire's published assertion that England was the most irreligious of countries, will not stand dispassionate examination. The clergy, it is true, judged as a body, were held in contempt ; but Christianity itself, though, as Bishop Secker complained in 1738, " railed at and ridiculed with very little reserve " in certain intellectual quarters, still claimed the allegiance of the people. In London and many provincial towns the lecture-ships, founded in Puritan times and largely held by Evangelicals, still drew large congregations. Of Melmoth's *Great Importance of a Religious Life*, published in 1711, no fewer than 42,000 copies were sold within a few years. Deism, though popular at court and with the educated few, had no footing among the masses or with the country squires. In diverse ways, both in the university and elsewhere, thoughtful men were feeling out towards something less arid than the current beliefs—not always wisely, as we see from the curious story of the Hutchinsonians.   Walpole and Bolingbroke and others of the governing classes might privately ridicule the religion to whose forms for political purposes they professed complete adherence, but after all this scepticism was one of the marks of a class, like the snuff-box or the powdered peruke, one of the many signs of the dangerous breach between the few and the many, the governing and the governed, the outcome of which, on the Continent, was the French Revolution, the result of which in England would have been the same dangerous outbreak, had it not been for the Methodist revival.

CHAPTER II

JOHN WESLEY

ARGUMENT

I

In this hour of sensual indifference, hard materialism and contented blindness, England was saved by one man, " A mighty leader who brought forth water from the rocks to make a barren land live again." [1] In John Wesley the opportunity found the hero. "It is prodigious," remarked Johnson once, "the quantity of good that may be done by one man if he will make a business of it." And throughout his long life Wesley certainly made this his one "business." In an age of indifference he was ever strenuous; amid the profound selfishness of the times he never spared himself. In return it was given him to see of the travail of his soul, and to rejoice in the "prodigious quantity of good" which he had been enabled to accomplish. "To thousands of men and women his preaching and gospel revealed a new heaven and a new earth; it brought religion into soulless lives and reconstituted it as a comforter, an inspiration, and a judge. No one was too poor, too humble, too degraded, to be born again and share in the privilege of divine grace, to serve the one Master, Christ, and to attain to this blessed fruition of God's peace. Aloof alike from politics and the speculations of the schools, Wesley wrestled with the evils of his day and proclaimed the infinite power of a Christian faith based on personal conviction, eternally renewed from within, to battle with sin, misery and vice in all its forms." The social service that he accomplished was not the least of his triumphs.

[1] H. W. Temperley in *Camb. Mod. Hist.*, vi. 16.

For Methodism diverted into religious channels a vast volume of social discontent, which in France swelled the tides that in 1789 submerged Church and State.[1] Of even greater importance is it to remember the new elements of moral and religious influence which he gave to the English people at the beginning of an era of imperial expansion.

Of the greatness of Wesley there can be no question. A sufficient monument of his greatness, for those who would look around, will be found in the organised millions of adherents of the Methodist Church among the English-speaking races of all lands. " I consider him," wrote Southey in 1818, " the most influential mind of the last century." In 1879 he was described by Gladstone as " that extraordinary man whose life and acts have taken their place in the religious history, not only of England, but of Christendom." " In the many-sidedness of his education, and in his unwearied interest in all branches of knowledge "—we quote the verdict of one of the foremost scholars of Germany, Dr Loofs of Halle—" he is without a peer among revival preachers in any age." According to J. R. Green, " he embodied in himself not this or that side of the vast (Methodist) movement, but the very movement itself." " If ever there was a poor, fallible man," writes Canon Overton, " whose aims

[1] *Cf.* C. G. Robertson, *England under the Hanoverians*, p. 211.

were uniformly noble and disinterested, that man was John Wesley." " If the England of to-day," adds Cornelius de Witt, " no longer resembles the England of the eighteenth century, it is mainly due to him." To the same effect is the judgement of a recent historian. After pointing out the hard materialism of the eighteenth century, Mr Temperley reminds us that the eighteenth century was not without its rebels who " sought to dam or divert the streams of tendency. Of these men Chatham among politicians, Thomson among poets, Berkeley among philosophers, Law among divines, all derived new thoughts, evoked new harmonies, or caught new inspirations from the age. But more important than any of these in universality of influence, and in range of achievement, were John Wesley and the religious revival to which he gave his name and life." [1]

II

John Wesley was born on 17th June (O.S.) 1703 at Epworth rectory in Lincolnshire. By descent on both sides he came of a tough Nonconformist stock. His paternal great grandfather, Bartholomew Westley of Lyme Regis, was one of the clergy ejected in 1662 ; his grandfather was driven from place to

[1] *Cambridge Modern History,* vi. 77.

place under the infamous Five Mile Act ; while his grandmother's father, Mr White, was the chairman of the Westminster Assembly of Divines. But Wesley's father had early renounced Dissent, tramped to Oxford, and there become saturated with the prevalent High Church Toryism. Nevertheless, in spite of himself, we see the influence in Samuel Wesley of his Nonconformist ancestry and their beliefs. As he lay dying (1738) he told his son John : " The inward witness, son, the inward witness ! This is the proof, the strongest proof of Christianity." " I did not at the time understand them," adds John, when repeating the words long years afterwards.

More important than the influence upon John Wesley of his father, was that of his mother Susanna, to whom has been rightly given the title of " The mother of Methodism." All writers acknowledge that she was a woman of extraordinary intelligence and will, of somewhat Spartan instincts, totally destitute of humour, who carried method into everything, religion included. Her father was a distinguished Nonconformist divine, Dr Annesley, of Queen's College, Oxford, who, in 1662, was ejected from Cripplegate Church. From him she had inherited a character, the main traits of which, according to her son, were " her orderliness, reasonableness, steadfastness of purpose, calm authority, and tender affection." Her reading was extensive for the day, and shows the strong influence upon her of Pascal. At the age of thirteen she showed her force of will by renouncing her father's dissent, or rather the Socinianism into which she had reasoned herself. Her letters, especially her correspondence with her son John, show a deeply religious character, remarkable both for its insight, and for the way in which she succeeded in winning to herself the tender confidence of her sons. As the mother of nineteen children—of whom John was the eleventh,—as the partner of a somewhat impracticable poetaster, as the housewife who could never escape the burden of poverty—the total income of Epworth was less than £50 a year,—she needed to have all her wits about her ; all her bravery, too, to bear up against the tragedy of her daughters' marriages.

At the age of eleven Wesley entered Charterhouse as a gown-boy. There he remained six years. In 1719 his brother Samuel, who was then head usher of Westminster, writes to his father : " Jack is with me—a brave boy, learning Hebrew as fast as he can." In strenuousness, at any rate, the boy was father of the man. In spite of its rough lawlessness Wesley formed a high esteem of Charterhouse. " A public school," writes Wesley at a later date, " promises manly assurance, and an early knowledge of the ways of the world." In 1716 his brother Charles entered Westminster, and for four years the three brothers were in London together. But in 1720 John entered Christ Church, Oxford, his brother Charles following him six years later. In the eighteenth century Oxford was at the lowest point of the long degradation which had followed the Reformation. Its dreary hatred of all " enthusiasm " was not even redeemed by the twentieth-century cult of the athlete. Politically, Oxford had become identified with a sullen Jacobitism, and in consequence was fatally cut off from the currents of national life. Educationally, its influence was but slight, " casual, secondary, and incidental "— to quote the verdict of Mark Pattison. Wesley's judgement upon Oxford was almost as severe as that of Gibbon. He found that nothing was " so scarce as learning, save religion." The general idleness disgusted him ; the utter disregard of the statutes seemed to him immoral.

In 1726 Wesley was elected a fellow of Lincoln College, one of the few colleges that had not altogether yielded to the evil influences of the times. For a short time he held a curacy at Wroote, in his father's parish ; in November 1729 he returned to Lincoln to take up tutorial work. He lectured in Greek and logic. This last subject was always a favourite with him. " I praise God," he writes, " for giving me this honest art." His contemporary,

Gambold, supplies us with the reason. "The first thing Wesley struck at in young men was that indolence which would not submit to close thinking." His fidelity to his duties was marked. Wesley himself tells us that he would have thought himself "little better than a highwayman" if he had neglected his lectures; "learning on principle of conscience" was one of the matters that he sought to instil into his pupils.

Shortly after his return from Wroote, Wesley, who had come under the influence of Law's *Serious Call*, became the recognised leader in a little group in the University, already known as "Methodists," because they had "agreed together to observe with strict formality the method of study and practice laid down in the statutes." The number of members in this "Holy Club" fluctuated considerably. At the outside it numbered twenty-seven; once it sank to five. The founder of these Oxford "Methodists," "Sacramentarians," or "Bible Moths"—for their nicknames were many—was his brother Charles who, in 1726, had been elected a student of Christ Church. At that time Charles was "a sprightly, rollicking young fellow with more genius than grace." "What!" he retorted once to his brother's entreaties, "would you have me to be a saint all at once." But coming under deeper impressions he began to partake of the

Sacrament weekly in the College Chapel, and to induce two or three others to follow his example. Feeling the need of further guidance Charles consulted his brother John. " In November 1729," writes Wesley in his *Journal*, " four young gentlemen of Oxford, Mr John Wesley, Fellow of Lincoln College, Mr Charles Wesley, Student of Christ Church, Mr Morgan, Commoner of Christ Church, and Mr Kirkham, of Merton College, began to spend some evenings a week in reading, chiefly the New Testament." They also bound themselves to hold regular seasons for prayer, to the rigorous observance of the fasts of the Church, the use of the Confessional, a stern self-discipline, and systematic visitation of the sick and poor, as well as of the prisoners in Bocardo—the Oxford gaol. In a passionate enthusiasm for self-denial Wesley at this time found the mark of true religious life. " No man," he said, " is in a state of salvation until he is contemned by the whole world." In all essentials, in fact, the beginnings of the Oxford Movements of the eighteenth and nineteenth century were similar. In the long run also the leaders in both were driven out of the Church of England. But while for the most part the disciples of the Tractarians remained within the Anglican Church, the followers of Wesley were anxious for separation. But long before the separation came,

C

Wesley himself had abandoned most of his Oxford ideas.

Of the members of this " Holy Club " the best known, next to the Wesleys, was George Whitefield, though James Hervey, the author of the *Meditations among the Tombs*, and John Clayton, the Jacobite Rector of Manchester, should not be forgotten. As in the later Oxford movement Pusey and Keble remained when Newman left, so with the " Holy Club." Clayton and Hervey had no sympathy with the later developments into which Wesley was led. Comparisons with the Oxford Movement, though useful and necessary, break down in one matter. Newman and the Tractarians profoundly swayed the University ; there is little evidence that Wesley and his associates produced much impression upon the life of Oxford. The " Holy Club " would have been as ephemeral in its reputation as most other University societies, nor, for that matter, had it a much longer life than the majority. It owes its place in history solely to the after deeds of three of its members—Whitefield, and the two Wesleys.

In October 1735 John and Charles Wesley set off for America to convert the settlers and Indians in Oglethorpe's colony of Georgia. " My chief motive," John writes, " is the hope of saving my own soul." In words which would have charmed Rousseau, he dreamed of a return to nature as a return to grace. " I cannot hope," he said, " to attain the same degree of holiness here which I may there." The Wesleys were followed in 1737 by George Whitefield. This missionary journey must not be judged either by Wesley's motives, or by the apparent failure of the results. As with much else in the eighteenth century the event was greater than the age conceived. The missionary call—so long neglected by the Protestant Churches —was once more heard and obeyed. As we see from Bishop Berkeley's project for a college in Bermuda, from Codrington's College in the Barbadoes, from Colonel Spotswood's school for the education of Indians in Virginia, and from the mission in 1751 of the Society for the Propagation of the Gospel to the coast of Guinea, once more men began to dream of the world for Christ. In the mission to Georgia we have one of the beginnings of the great movement which, at a later date, received fuller organisation from Carey, Coke and other founders of modern missionary societies.

Wesley's mission, while of importance for the future, was, however, worse than a failure. Wesley, in Southey's words, instead of feeding his flock with milk, " drenched them with the physic of an intolerant discipline," of which, in after years, he was heartily ashamed, and which, at the time, led him into trouble. Throughout life, in his relations to women, Wesley displayed a " guileless simplicity." His later domestic life was spoiled by his shrewish wife ; his earlier career at Savannah was in danger of being wrecked by a romantic and painful love affair. In the upshot it led to his leaving Georgia. At the same time Charles ruined his career by a lack of tact which set even Oglethorpe against him.

Though the mission was a failure, the importance of the experience for the Wesleys, personally, was great. The journey had taught John—to quote his own words, about the truth of which, however, in later life he had many misgivings—" that I, who went to America to convert others, was never myself converted." The journey had also brought the brothers into touch with the Moravians. Through their leader, Peter Böhler, Wesley was led at last into spiritual rest. The first step was the conviction of " the want of faith whereby alone we are saved." From this stress and doubt Charles was the first who found deliverance, followed a few days later by his brother. On the evening of 24th May 1738, a day which marks, as Lecky says, " an epoch in English history," Wesley went, " very unwillingly," to a meeting of one of the " religious societies,"—an Anglican society be it noted, and not as is so often stated, a Moravian,—in Aldersgate Street, probably in Nettleton Court. Throughout the day he had been eagerly listening for some message. Now as he heard a member read Luther's *Preface to the Epistle to the Romans* :

"About a quarter before nine, while he was describing the change which God works in the heart through faith in Christ, I felt my heart strangely warmed. I felt I did trust in Christ alone for salvation, and an assurance was given me that he had taken away my sins."

On that day Methodism, as history knows it, was born, nor is it by accident that it was so strangely linked up in its birth with the great German reformer.

Into the precise meaning of Wesley's conversion, as a fact in his own spiritual history, we do not propose to enter. Without the throes of a great spiritual struggle, no great religious leader has ever reached the clear consciousness of his spiritual mission. St Paul, St Augustine, St Francis, Luther, Bunyan—the name is legion—all alike illustrate this fundamental fact. Most of those who have passed through such fires are somewhat prone to undervalue their previous experiences, or to exaggerate the suddenness of the transition. Wesley was no exception to the rule, though, in his later years, he formed a much more charitable view of the value of his earlier religious life than in the first enthusiasm of his conversion. Most men to-day would agree with Canon Overton's criticism of Wesley's excessive self-condemnation : " If John Wesley was not a true Christian (when in Georgia), God help millions of those who profess and call themselves Christians." But be this as it may, of the importance as a landmark in the history of Protestant Christianity of this " conversion " there can be no doubt. The Wesley of the " Holy Club " and of Georgia would scarcely have secured the humblest mention even in the most comprehensive Dictionary of National Biography. It was " that wonderful experience " in Aldersgate Street that has given to the name of John Wesley its place in the history of Christendom. Henceforth, for half a century—we quote his letter to Walker of Truro— he had but :

> " One point in view—to promote so far as I am able, vital, practical religion, and by the grace of God, to beget, preserve, and increase the life of God in the souls of men."

How well and faithfully he carried out his ideal is known of all men. Upon the details of that wonderful life we shall not dwell, if only because every student should read them for himself as set forth by Wesley in his *Journals*—one of the most valuable human documents of any age, indispensable for all

who would understand the England of the eighteenth
century, or the life and labours of its great apostle.
In the heat of summer, in the snows of winter ;
exposed to discomforts of all sorts and dangers not
a few, by day or night ; along roads infested with
robbers, so bad that three days was a fair allowance
for a ride from London to Bristol ; losing his way
on the mountains, detained at the ferries for hours,
overtaken by the dark where there was no shelter
but the meanest hovel ; through the length and
breadth of England, Scotland and Ireland John
Wesley incessantly journeyed, never travelling less,
as he tells us, than "four thousand five hundred
miles in a year" ; reading as he went; writing, as
he rested, tracts and polemics, or abridging the best
literature for his people ; preaching everywhere,
whether the people were anxious to hear him or
had been kindled into a furious mob that sought his
life, indifferent whether it were to half a dozen in
some tiny room, or to the thousands that thronged
around him on Moorfields or Kennington ; with
the care upon him of all his churches, and the
numberless details, neither relinquished nor over-
looked, which the affairs of a growing society
involved.

On Wednesday, 2nd March 1791, Wesley passed
away amidst the tears and songs of those who had
loved and reverenced him as their father in God.

The last sentence he had recorded in his *Journal* is in one sense characteristic of his whole life : " For upwards of eighty-six years I have kept my accounts exactly : I will not attempt it any longer, being satisfied with the continual conviction that I save all I can and give all I can ; that is, all I have." Five months before the end he had preached his last sermon in the open air at Winchester, from the text, The Kingdom of Heaven is at hand. " The tears of the people," writes one who was present, " flowed in torrents." Though manifestly feeble he toiled on to the end, planning a round of visits to the West of England which he did not live to fulfil. On 23rd February, he preached his last sermon in the magistrates' room at Leatherhead. A few days later he was not, for God took him. Almost his last words were a shout of victory, " The best of all is God is with us ! "

III

Hitherto we have said nothing as to Wesley's co-workers and helpers. Lack of space, and not the measure of their deserts, compels us to brevity. Whitefield, the great orator of Methodism, was for a long time, by a curious lack of historical perspective, regarded as the head of the revival, compared with whom Wesley was but of secondary importance.

That a truer estimate is now current of his real
position must not lead us to overlook the greatness
of his labours. Born in 1714, in the Bell Inn, at
Gloucester, in 1732 Whitefield entered Pembroke
College, Oxford, as a servitor, and was there at once
brought into touch with the " Holy Club," so far
as his humbler opportunities allowed. In 1736
he was ordained a deacon and preached his first
sermon, the effect of which was that he was reported
to his bishop for driving fifteen people mad.
Though only twenty-two his success was instant and
phenomenal. In Bristol the churches were crowded
twice every day of the week to hear him ; in London
he was forced to ride by coach to his services to
escape the attentions of the people. After a year
in Georgia he was back again in London, and in
1739 was ordained a priest. Finding the doors
of the churches closed against him, he was the first
to take a bold step, the influence of which on the
fortunes of the revival cannot be exaggerated.
On 17th February 1739, he cast all scruples aside
and preached out of doors to a congregation of two
hundred colliers on Kingswood Hill, near Bristol.
Within a few days the congregation had grown
into thousands. Though only a return to the
methods of St Francis of Assisi, of Wyclif's Bible-
men, and of other medieval preachers, this departure
from dull convention aroused bitter opposition.

Within one year forty-nine pamphlets and burlesques were published against the author of this innovation.

In August 1739 Whitefield sailed a second time to America. In Philadelphia and New York he carried all before him, and powerfully prepared the way for the more enduring labours of the Methodist pioneers who followed him. As Whittier has finely expressed it in his poem of *The Preacher* :

> " The flood of emotion, deep and strong,
> Troubled the land as it swept along,
> But left a result of holier lives."

From this time onwards, Whitefield, whether back again in the old country, or across the seas in the new continent, led the life of a clerical free-lance somewhat hampered by holy orders. His oratory, the secret of which is not revealed by any of his published works, with their manifest absence both of culture and thought, influenced all classes ; it could charm the cynical Horace Walpole, wring gold from the close-fisted Benjamin Franklin, awaken envy in Garrick, move the cold, sceptical Hume to admiration, and at the same time cause the tears to stream down the sooty faces of the Kingswood miners. Whatever may have been his gifts of voice or manner the real soul of his influence must be found in the intense reality of his sympathy

with the sins and sorrows of the human heart.
" If ever," writes Sir James Stephen, " philanthropy burned in the human heart with a pure and
intense flame embracing the whole family of man
in the spirit of universal charity, it was in the heart
of George Whitefield. He loved the world that
hated him. He had no preferences but in favour
of the ignorant, the miserable, and the poor. In
their cause he shrunk from no privation, and declined
neither insult nor hostility." [1] After thirty-one years
of restless energy, during which he preached 18,000
sermons, and crossed the Atlantic thirteen times,
he passed away to his reward at Newbury Port in
America (30th September 1770). His funeral
sermon at Tottenham Court Road Chapel was
preached by John Wesley. The two friends,
severed for a while by the bitter Calvinistic controversy, were now one. " Have we read or heard,"
asked Wesley, " of any person since the apostles who
testified the Gospel of the Grace of God through
so large a part of the habitable world ? Have we
read or heard of any person who called so many
thousands, so many myriads of sinners to repent-
ance ? Above all, have we heard or read of anyone
who has been a blessed instrument in the hands
of God of bringing so many sinners from darkness
to light, and from the power of Satan unto God ? "

[1] *Essays in Ecclesiastical Biography*, p. 387.

Of more permanent importance than Whitefield, from the standpoint of Methodism and its future, was Charles Wesley, who was born at Epworth on 18th December 1707. For long years he and his brother John, though they had seen little of each other in early life, were one alike in their aims, their methods, and in the intensity with which they threw themselves into their work. But towards the end of life they drifted somewhat apart, as Charles perceived more clearly than John the inevitable tendency of the societies towards separation from the Anglican Church, and especially the bearing of John's ordinations. His happy marriage in 1749 had also caused Charles to retire from his former constant itinerancy, and to settle down, first at Bristol, and afterwards (1771) in Marylebone. Thus he grew out of touch both with the Methodist preachers and with the work in general, apart from the London societies. To these last he ministered to the end, being especially assiduous in his attentions to the prisoners of Newgate. He died on 29th May 1788 and was buried, at his own request, in Marylebone Parish Church.

Of John's power of organisation Charles showed but little sign. Nor did he share in his brother's intensely practical outlook, with its consequent determination to subordinate the theoretically perfect to the main end. But the value of the work of Charles as the " sweet singer " of the movement cannot be exaggerated. " Long hence, when possibly the standard works of the elder brother are read only by the preachers, and the organisation which he built up has been so modified as to show but little trace of its original form, the hymns of Charles Wesley will continue to permeate the Methodist Church with the gracious leaven of its primitive experience." [1] For the people the creed of Methodism is expressed rather in the hymns of Charles than in the standard sermons of John Wesley. The hymns rather than the sermons have preserved the unity of belief. They have served, in fact, as a lyric *credo*, the expression in song of the faith of our fathers. The evangelical revival and its spirit throbs through them all; they are instinct with the conception of the personal experience of religion; their constant proclamation is the universality of salvation; their constant witness is to the Methodist doctrines of perfect love and assurance. At the same time, they present a full embodiment of the Person and Work both of the Redeemer and of the Holy Spirit. Nor, in their original forms, are the hymns of Charles Wesley uncertain in their emphasis of the importance and objective value of the Sacraments of the Church.

There are few blessings which have not some dis-

[1] F. L. Wiseman in *New History of Methodism*, i. 242.

advantages. The greatness of Charles Wesley as a hymn-writer, the stately translations, especially from the German, of the elder brother, and the unrivalled lyrics of Watts, upon which Wesley had freely drawn in the preparation of his hymn books, led to a remarkable barrenness in later years in the Methodist Church · itself. Two or three of the Methodist preachers had indeed contributed to the early hymn books, among whom mention should be made of John Bakewell, the author of " Hail, thou once despised Jesus," and of Thomas Olivers who, in 1774, composed the majestic ode, " The God of Abraham praise." Nor must we forget Edward Perronet, who, for some years joined John Wesley in his journeys, and whose hymn " All hail the power of Jesu's name " has become a universal favourite. But with the eighteenth century, Methodist song died away. While other churches were pouring forth their deepest thoughts and feelings in inspired verse, the Methodist Conferences, at any rate in the Old World, allowed their reverence for the priceless treasure bequeathed to them from the past to become a snare. The hymn book was stereotyped, and only through unofficial channels could the great modern hymns, e.g., those of Faber and Newman, find their way into popular use. No provision was made for the more recent developments of church life and thought, or for the growing consciousness of national problems and needs. This much may be said, for this excessive conservatism, that it kept out of the Methodist Church much that was ephemeral and unworthy ; at the same time, it preserved many hymns of Charles Wesley that had long since become unreal, whether because of their diffuse allegorism, or because of their excessive subjectivity. But from this danger, as recent hymn books both in England and America show, Methodism is now delivered. In the range and catholicity of its song the Methodist Church to-day still possesses its most effective appeal to the spiritual.

But we must return to our more immediate theme. Of Wesley's co-workers mention must be made of John Fletcher of Madeley, a naturalised Swiss whom Wesley intended to be his successor. The character of this singularly saintly man is said to have won the admiration of Voltaire ; we need not wonder, therefore, that Wesley found in him the completest embodiment of what he meant by his doctrine of entire sanctification. As a theological writer, Fletcher exercised considerable influence, especially by his exposure of the current antinomian tendencies. Though he did not join Wesley in his ceaseless itineration, he was yet throughout life one of the few Anglican clergy who understood John Wesley, and sympathised fully with his methods and aims.

Others there were of whom much might be said,

did space allow. Of these, the most prominent was Selina, Countess of Huntingdon (1707-91), who made it her life business to bring about a revival among the upper classes, and whose zeal in building chapels of ease, which she supplied with evangelical clergy of her own appointment, led to her becoming registered as a dissenter, against her will. Of the men whom Wesley trained, mention must be made, in addition to Thomas Olivers, of John Haime who introduced Methodism into the British army, and of John Nelson, the stonemason of Birstall who was illegally pressed for a soldier in order to stop his preaching. But neither pressgangs nor mobs could silence him; persecution was powerless against his serenity of soul. In Bradford he was flung into a filthy cell. "My soul," he writes, in words which remind us of a similar utterance of Jacopone da Todi, the author of "Stabat Mater," "was so filled with the love of God, that it was a paradise to me. I wished my enemies were as happy in their own houses, as I was in the dungeon." Of a younger generation, we should not forget Samuel Bradburn, a great orator who was, however, sadly lacking in self-control, and Joseph Benson, who, though the most scholarly of Wesley's itinerants, was a most impassioned revivalist.

IV

To two or three distinctive features of Wesley's wonderful life, special attention should be drawn. When John Wesley said that the world was his parish, he pointed to the secret both of his success and of the antagonism which he aroused. In the England of the eighteenth century, localism was intense, the counterpart of the selfish individualism which was the bane of the age. Religious life was intensely parochial. The episcopate itself was local, each bishop doing what he deemed to be right, without consultation with his brethren or with his archbishop. And here was a man, who not only set at nought all the rules and regulations of parochialism, glorying in this breach of ecclesiastical discipline (of the nature of which he seems to have been completely unconscious), urging that the supreme need of the day, was that others should follow his example. Add to this the plain, outspoken words which touched men in their tenderest spot—their pride in their respectable but lifeless Christianity,—or roused men to opposition by the fearlessness which condemned their darling or most profitable sins, and we need not wonder that the mobs which assailed him were too often stirred up by the parson or squire.

Very noteworthy, especially when account is

D

taken of the other extraordinary activities of his
life, is the use that Wesley made of his pen. In this
to some extent he was the child of his age. The
early years of the eighteenth century were remarkable for an extraordinary multiplication of pamphlets
published at low prices and reaching in some cases
a gigantic circulation. As a rule, these pamphlets
were political. What Wesley did was to use the
current taste for cheap literature for the promulga-
tion of the articles of his faith. He filled the saddle-
bags of his itinerant preachers with cheap books,
including tracts, written in terse, logical English, and
abbreviations of the great masterpieces of literature. Though Wesley seems to have been strangely
ignorant of the life and work of Wyclif, the later
reformer, in his constant appeal to the pen, followed
in the footsteps of the great medieval pamphleteer.

We must not overlook another special cause of
Wesley's success. We have noted already that in
the eighteenth century the Church had substituted
for doctrinal teaching, the emphasis of a moral
code. Wesley discerned the great truth—borne out
by the experience of centuries, that the highest
morality can only be founded upon a supernatural
i.e., a doctrinal basis. He saw that to make morality
the end instead of the consequence leads to disaster ;
that the mere washing of the cup and the platter
does not give moral purification. He insisted upon

going back to first principles, upon laying the
foundation deep in the facts of the soul ; the rest
would follow as inevitably as daylight follows the
dawn. And history once more showed the old
lesson to which the Butlers and Clarks had been
curiously blind, the lesson that in every century has
to be learned afresh—that the great doctrines are not
dogmas of the intellect but fountains in the soul
which well up into the most beautiful lives. Methodism once more demonstrated, as Nicea had demonstrated in earlier days, that the dynamic of life
lies in a great conviction, and that, to reach the
people, such conviction must be stated in simple
language, without subtle reservations and explana-
tions, by those who make it manifest by their deeds
that they believe the doctrines which they preach.

A word should be said as to the relation of Wesley
to the thought of the age.[1] Some writers have spoken
of Methodism as the swing of the pendulum from the
intellectual to the emotional side of Christianity ;
as a reaction against the tendency so manifest in the
Apologists, to view Christianity almost exclusively
from the standpoint of reason. But this is to do an
injustice to Wesley. Throughout his life the " some-
time fellow of Lincoln College, Oxford," tried to keep
himself in touch with the intellectual movements of

[1] On this matter I may refer the reader to the fuller analysis I
have given in *A New History of Methodism*, i. c. 1.

his age, and, considering his busy life, his success
in this respect was remarkable. He never under-
valued either scholarship or culture. In his *Earnest
Appeal to Men of Reason* he refused to be misled by
the specious reasoning of Dodwell (1742) that
" Christianity is not founded on argument." But,
on the other hand, he never made the mistake into
which the Deists fell, of regarding the unassisted
reason as sufficient for all human needs, thus con-
fusing knowledge and life. For him, knowledge
was only the auxiliary of love, and knowledge without
love, however orthodox, was only a " dead empty
form void of spirit and faith." A Christianity without practical influence might be proved on paper beyond dispute, and yet from the complete absence
of all driving power be as logically denied. He was
convinced that the best apology for Christianity
would be found in its deeds, that a Church girded
with strength need not trouble overmuch about the
attacks on its minor fortifications. Like Napoleon,
he believed that the secret of effective defence lay
in assuming the aggressive in the enemy's country.

Nevertheless, the Methodist movement cannot be
altogether disassociated from the thought of the
times. If in some of its aspects Methodism may seem
to be a reaction against the age, yet in others Wesley
was more influenced than he was himself aware of
by the *Zeitgeist*. We see this especially in the

characteristic feature of the movement—Wesley's appeal to experience.

The appeal of philosophy to experience, had originated with Des Cartes. In this matter, as in some of its issues, Cartesianism was the philosophical counterpart of the Reformation. Oxford, it is true, following the lead of the Jesuits, had banned Cartesianism. As a consequence the extension by Malebranche of Cartesian doctrine into the mystical vision of all things in God had failed to establish itself in the university of Wesley. Instead, English philosophy had developed the Cartesian argument on lines of reaction peculiar to itself, and, under the lead of Hobbes and Locke, had twisted the whole matter into a question of deductive psychology. In introspection, the examination of the contents of the mind and feelings, they had endeavoured to find the grounds of validity of thought and being. Such an effort was bound to lead to nescience, as indeed we see when Hume with unflinching logic, carried out the promises of Locke and Hobbes to their legitimate conclusion. Introspection cannot but end, as he showed, in the demonstration of its own impotence. The analysis of the mind, viewed as the sole sufficient organon of truth, resolves all into fleeting sensations in which we can find neither permanence of the ego, nor warrant of belief in aught objective, whether God, morality, or self. The "waking" of Kant from his " dogmatic slumbers " saved philosophy from the *impasse* into which the English school had thus led it.

But we are anticipating. Wesley himself knew little of Hume and nothing of Kant. The *Zeitgeist* influenced him before Hume had shown its logical issue, or Kant pointed out the more excellent way. Nevertheless, in any survey of English thought, the place of Wesley cannot be neglected. For his appeal to experience was not " mere enthusiasm," as Warburton and other writers of the eighteenth century urged, still less was it the outcome of a mysticism which Wesley but imperfectly apprehended. In his appeal he was one, however unconsciously, with the English philosophers, with one all-important difference. The philosophers had confined themselves almost exclusively to the intellectual factors. Wesley urged, though not, of course, in so many words, an enlargement so as to embrace spiritual phenomena of the contents of mind to which the philosophers applied their method of introspection. In modern terms Wesley claimed that spiritual phenomena have a reality of their own, which neither scientist nor psychologist can ignore, and which is in itself its own sufficient warrant.

Methodism, the child of the eighteenth century, was subject, as might naturally be expected, at any

rate, in its early days, to many of the limitations
of the century. For instance, the eighteenth
century was curiously blind to the meaning of
childhood ; in this respect it differed in nothing
from the centuries before it. In consequence, the
Methodist revival displayed neither sympathy with
nor understanding of the life and soul of the child.
Wesley's methods of training at his famous Kingswood School, his refusal to allow either play or
holidays, his dictum that " he who will play as a
boy, will play as a man," his rigid conceptions of
total depravity in its application to childhood, the
absence from his services of all hymns either for
children or that children could understand, or of
any provision to meet their special needs, all seem
strange to an age that has specialised in child-
study. But in reality in these matters Wesley
differed little from the general thought of his day,
except in his clearness of expression, and his greater
insistence upon the value of education and of the
strenuous life. Among the unrealised dreams of
history, we may wonder at the difference that would
have been made in the welfare of our own country
if Wesley had understood children, and, with a
heart as tender as St Anselm's or St Francis', had
tried to meet their needs. The hideous horrors
of child-labour which, in the next century, wrung
from Mrs Browning, Dickens, and others, their

noble protests, the general indifference to education which until 1870, doomed the major part of the children to ignorance, the rigidity and repression of child-religion except it took certain severe and conventional forms, in a words all the trouble of the children from the accumulations of which we are only slowly and with difficulty freeing ourselves in the twentieth century, might either have been prevented or their problems solved a century earlier.

Yet even in this matter, undoubted as was Wesley's weakness, we may discover some germs of better things. Wesley's mistakes at his Kingswood School need not be minimised ; at the same time, it were well to remember how he stood out above his age in his insistence upon the strenuous life at school. The schools of the times, even the best of them, woefully failed to accomplish the purpose of their founders. The idleness of the boys, the incapacity of the ushers, the selfish greed which diverted foundations to other purposes, and, if we may trust Cowper and others, the immorality of the schools was notorious. In his reaction from general rottenness, Wesley undoubtedly swung to the opposite extreme. Nevertheless the attempt, as the distinguished history for now nearly two centuries of Kingswood School has abundantly shown, was not without its value.

Nor must we forget that as one result of the

Evangelical revival we have the foundation by
Robert Raikes of Gloucester (1780) of the Sunday
School, on the lines of previous attempts. In their
early forms, and for long afterwards, Sunday Schools,
it is true, showed little clear apprehension of either
the needs of children, or of their special work in the
Church. Sunday Schools were generally regarded
as outside the Church, at the best its flying buttresses,
never as an integral, necessary part of the adaptation of the Gospel to varying conditions. Moreover,
they were hampered at every turn by the ignorance
of the children, who could neither read nor write.
But the fact that the problem of the Sunday
School was neither quickly apprehended nor quickly
solved—for that matter the twentieth century is
still seeking the right solution,—nor that, in many
quarters, the whole movement was looked upon with
suspicion, should blind us to the great advance
that was made.

V

The student who ponders the origin and history
of religious revivals, will note the absence from them,
as a rule, of all deliberate constructive statesmanship.
Politics may find a place for the Abbè Sieyès, with
his endless schemes of constitutions, or for a Richelieu
with his plan of reconstruction. In the great affairs
of the soul men are led by the Spirit of God. Neither

St Paul, nor St Francis, nor Luther, were conscious, when they set out, of the end of their journey. Among great leaders in the Church, Hildebrand and Calvin alone stand out as men who imaged the whole, before they executed the parts. Wesley was no exception to the general rule. To compare him, as does Lord Macaulay, with Richelieu, because of his genius for organisation, is to miss the essential difference between the two men. With Richelieu organisation was a deliberate purpose and ideal ; with Wesley it was an incident into which he was driven, oftentimes, as in the case of his lay preachers, in spite of himself. In his powers of organisation Wesley would be better compared with another great Englishman of kindred temperament. Like Cromwell, Wesley possessed a firm grasp upon the facts of life, and a rare power of shaping into in-stitutions the religious emotions which might other-wise have exhausted themselves in momentary enthusiasm. As with Cromwell, so with Wesley, there was, in consequence, a certain opportunism, the result of practical necessities, which led them both to set at nought laws and regulations to which in heart they were perfectly loyal.

We have said that Wesley set at nought the rules and regulations of his Church, while Whitefield's offences were even more flagrant. Whether these breaches of discipline were justified or not, is not

now the question ; that they existed can scarcely
be denied by impartial critics. We should do injustice to Wesley's character, if we attributed this
to design, or to a lack of appreciation of scholarship
or order. By nature, Wesley was given rather to
the trodden paths than to the discovery of new
routes. With impulse and enthusiasm his cold,
keen intellect had few affinities ; his habits and
temperament inclined him to the hatred of all
irregularities, whether in dress, conduct, or religion.
Nothing is more remarkable than the fact, that such
a man was driven into irregularity in spite of himself. But his very irregularities were a proof both of
his administrative genius, and of the intensity of his
convictions. Like Oliver Cromwell, with whom
we have already compared him, he was less concerned
with the means, provided he deemed them righteous,
than with the end ; like Oliver he was driven, in order
that he might attain the end, to the use of means
alien to his nature. He subordinated everything,
training, instincts, prejudices, to the accomplishment
of his great object, or rather to the fulfilment of his
imperative call. So, when driven out of the parish
churches, he reluctantly followed Whitefield and
took to field-preaching ; when the clergy forsook
him, he fell back upon lay preachers ; when America
could not obtain episcopal oversight, and the needs
of his new societies called, he ordained bishops

himself. With him the supreme need was the interests of the kingdom of God ; all else, however dear or desirable in itself, became secondary. There was, in Wesley, none of that obstinacy in the maintenance of custom or prepossession which is generally the mark of a mind unaccustomed to calculate real values, or to give to means and ends their proper proportions. Nor must we forget that the High Church party in the eighteenth century, to which by training and instinct, Wesley belonged, while making much of episcopacy as an abstract doctrine, were noted for their constant defiance of their ecclesiastical superiors—one of the many results of the political separation between the higher and lower clergy.

The student inquiring into the causes which led to the separation of Methodism from the Established Church, will thus discern on both sides the lack of design or insight so characteristic of the eighteenth century. Separation was certainly not the intention of the bishops ; they simply drifted on, and such action as they took, was marked rather by indifference than open hostility. So also with Wesley. Not without cause has he been likened to a rower whose face is set one way, but whom stream and effort alike, carry in an opposite direction. In spite of his passionate devotion to the Church of his father, he plunged into acts and deeds which were logically bound to end in the separation he dreaded. His institution of lay preachers, under the supervision of a wiser episcopate, might have been successfully grafted on to the Church ; his Conferences might have been developed as a substitute for the silenced Convocation ; his society classes did not differ organically from the Anglican societies of the day. Nevertheless, owing to hostility, lack of management, and general indifference, each of the great features of the new society became forces in the disruptive process. This was completed by Wesley's momentous action in claiming that a presbyter was the equal of a bishop, and had in consequence, the right of ordination of a bishop. This right he exercised, first for America in 1784,[1] and afterwards for Scotland. Though Charles Wesley was aware of the seriousness of the step, John himself seems to have been unconscious that thereby he had made separation inevitable. Moreover, even if he had been so conscious, his old love of regularity had long since given place to a determination to judge everything by its practical worth, in making for what he deemed to be righteousness, and in ministering to the interests of his organisation. That in an age saturated with individualism and egoism, both in politics, philosophy and commerce, Wesley in his actions, should be a complete in-

[1] See *infra*, p. 73.

dividualist—we are writing from what would be, as we deem, the standpoint of a thoughtful Anglican " catholic "—need excite no wonder ; the only marvel is that he should have considered his individualism to be reconcilable with his High Church principles. Add also that this individualistic outlook was united with constant insistence in his societies upon discipline and obedience, and the contradiction is complete.

To point out the unconscious drift of the whole movement is one thing ; to claim, as do some writers, that Methodism need never have separated from the Church is another. The answer to this last question will largely depend upon other considerations. On analysis these resolve themselves into a circle. From a Church wisely organised and wisely governed, in which the supreme interest had been the welfare of the Kingdom of God, Methodism need never have separated ; on the other hand, if such a Church had existed in England in the eighteenth century, Methodism would never have arisen. We may further grant that if the Church of England had been the Church of Rome, there would have been no separation. The genius of Rome, even in the darkest days of degradation, has always enabled it to utilise any movement of reform and turn it to account generally by organising it as a subordinate society. It was so in the thirteenth century with St Francis

of Assisi ; it was so in a later age with the followers
of Loyola. But for reasons into which we cannot
now enter, Protestantism, in all its different forms,
has never shown this capacity for dealing with
difference within its borders. There are signs, on
all hands, that the Protestant churches to-day
are awake to this defect in their genius ; but the
Church of England in the eighteenth century was
neither conscious of inadequacy nor, if it had been
so conscious, did it possess at that time the means
of cure. Only by the vigorous blood-letting, first of
the Methodist revival, then of the Oxford secessions
of Newman and others, was it driven in upon the
Anglican Church that her welfare did not lie in
securing artificial uniformity, whether by act of
Parliament or through episcopal unwillingness to
face new situations. The bane of eighteenth-century
individualism, the curse of its indifferentism, the
effects of its narrow visionlessness, could not be
escaped, nor without pain could a larger life be won.
John Wesley seems to have been one of the few men
who did not see that his reformation, in the then
constitution of the English Church, was really revolution, and could only be comprehended within
the Church by its being so successful that its
opponents would have become, virtually, nonconformists. The ideal and meaning of religion,
as set forth by Wesley, and as held by the better

type of eighteenth-century Anglicans, *e.g.* by Butler, were fundamentally opposite ; and it is useless, as well as unhistorical, for theorists to ignore the differences, or to point out the might-have-beens that would have followed from their imaginative reconstructions.

Though Wesley and his followers were driven from the English Church, his influence upon it was not altogether lost. There was, it is true, no immediate improvement ; if anything, the first result was rather the hardening of thought and life by the violent hostility which he excited. Even the Evangelicals, though at first they had sympathised with Wesley and thrown open to him their pulpits, drifted off into opposition, largely as the result of the unfortunate Calvinistic controversy. But when the first bitterness was past, we can see in the later Evangelical movement, the centre of which was at Clapham, and the influence of which upon the Church was so prominent in the early years of the nineteenth century, the result of his teaching, above all of his life and example ; the application also of some of his methods by men who, unlike Wesley himself, remained within the Church, or who, like Joseph Milner, disowned Methodism altogether. In another direction we note also influence of a more permanent character. Hitherto in the Church of England the " quires and places where they sing " had been rare and poor ; hymns formed no authorised part of its services. Tate and Brady, Sternhold and Hopkins, still reigned supreme. But the burst of song which accompanied the great revival could not fail to produce its effects on others. The dreary services that had been the rule both with Dissenters and the Establishment, gave place to brighter and more emotional forms of worship. The ministry of song, so marked a feature in every great spiritual up-heaval, once more regained her own.

The importance of Wesley's political influence cannot be exaggerated. In himself he was a curious mixture of critical independence and partisan Toryism. Of Wesley we may say with Green that " no man ever stood at the head of a great revolu-tion, whose temper was so anti-revolutionary." He believed in the divine right of kings. For the revolt of America, he condemned unsparingly the colonists, instead of the obstinacy of George III. and his ministers. At the same time he was before his age in his opposition to the slave-trade—that " execrable sum of all villanies " as he termed it,— and in his exposure of the evil effects of absenteeism in Ireland. The effects of his strong conservatism was apparent in the leanings of many of his followers. When, at the death of Wesley, the great shock of the French Revolution broke upon the world, the Methodists from the first ranged themselves against

E

it. If the Methodist revival had been led by a revolutionary leader, the Revolution would have swept England from end to end ; as it was, we had instead a dreary Tory reaction, the only justification for whose excesses was that England was fighting for her life. But disastrous as was the reaction, there can be little doubt but that the revolutionary spirit would have been more disastrous still. From this England was saved, not so much by the philippics of Burke as by the life and teaching of Wesley. When he saved the souls of the masses, he at the same time preserved the existing framework of society.

Nevertheless the social effect of the Methodist revival, especially if we link with it the Evangelical Movement, were most marked. In this connection, we may mention the checking of gambling by legislation, the greater strictness of Sunday observance, the suppression of duelling, a more sober style of dress, and an antipathy to theatre-going on the part of the serious—in other words, the general emergence once more of the old Puritan spirit. In some directions the revival broke new ground. Until 1750, the slave trade had received national encouragement and subsidies, and had been described in official documents as "most beneficial to this island." But the awakened religious consciousness could no longer condone its "execrable villanies," and in 1787, a committee was formed for the abolition of the trade. The Sunday Schools, established by Robert Raikes of Gloucester, marked the beginnings of a new interest in education, as we see, despite their limited range, in the schools started by Hannah More at Cheddar in 1789, and in the pupil-teacher systems inaugurated by Bell and Lancaster. With passionate human sympathy, John Howard, following out more fully the line of reform first sketched by James Oglethorpe, devoted himself to the cause of prisoner and debtor, visiting personally every English gaol, and forcing upon the country the consideration of the reformation both of prisons and of criminals. In many directions we see the rise of a broad, generous philanthropy, and of a civic and national consciousness of wrongs that must be righted.

CHAPTER III

METHODISM IN AMERICA AND BEYOND THE SEAS

I

In the following chapter we propose to deal with
the evolution of Methodism from a local society
into a world-wide Church, with roots planted deep
in every continent. Naturally we shall commence
with the United States. As in England, so in
America, the opportunity of Methodism was largely
due to the neglect of Anglicanism. Anglicanism
has always regarded Episcopacy as an integral part
of her Church life, but in her treatment of her
American churches the Church of England demon-

68

strated that for all practical purposes bishops might
be dispensed with. In some of the States, also,
originally settled by Congregationalists or Presby-
terians, the introduction of bishops would have led
to serious disturbance ; the colonists had been
driven out of the Old World by the bishops ; they
did not intend to suffer from them in the New.
But even in States where the Anglican Church was
established and endowed, the political exigencies
of the home Government would not allow of any
appointment of colonial bishops, in spite of the
appeals of colonial clergy and the efforts of the
missionary societies at home. The War of Independence increased the difficulties by making impossible
even such oversight as had hitherto existed on the
part of the Bishop of London and his commissaries.
But George III was as obstinate as usual, and
absolutely refused to allow of any episcopal ordination. Not until 1784, could the Anglicans obtain
the consecration of Seabury, and that only, by
means of the Scottish Episcopalians. But the
Anglican Church was never able to recover the
ground that it had lost. The States were ready to
receive any Church that would subordinate politics
and red tape to the great spiritual needs of the new
populations.

And this Methodism was abundantly prepared
to do. Methodism owes its introduction to the New

World to an Irishman, Philip Embury, who in 1766, began to hold meetings in his own house at New York; but its real history commenced with the preaching of Captain Thomas Webb, "soldier of the Cross, and spiritual son of John Wesley," whom President Adams described as a " most eloquent man." As the work grew, in 1768 a request was made to Wesley, to send " an able and experienced preacher ; a man of wisdom, of sound faith, and a good disciplinarian ; one whose heart and soul are in the work." To this Macedonian cry, Wesley replied at the Leeds Conference in 1769, by sending Richard Boardman and Joseph Pilmore, and collecting £20 for their expenses. In 1771, five others volunteered, among them the heroic Francis Asbury, to whose devotion and organising skill American Methodism will always owe an incalculable debt.

With the arrival of these pioneers, Methodism steadily progressed, in spite of the disasters of the War of Independence, of the suspicions excited by Wesley's *Calm Address to the American Colonies*, and by the indiscreet loyalty of some of the English ministers. So bitter was the temper of the times, that even native-born Methodists were tarred and feathered as, of necessity, belonging to a " tory " organisation. Even Asbury was compelled to go into retirement. But with the declaration of peace in 1783 the work greatly revived. A heroic band of pioneers penetrated everywhere, following the emigrants in their perilous journeys towards Kentucky, Ohio or Indiana, preaching to the little groups of squatters and settlers in the trackless forests, or on the great plains, oftentimes in danger of their lives from the Indians, more often in want of the barest necessaries. The historians of the United States have not always recognised the debt their country owes to these humble toilers. But for the zeal of these Methodist pioneers many thousands of the settlers would have had no religious instruction whatever. Nor were their services limited to preaching the gospel. They laid the foundations of commonwealths as they " inculcated respect for law, and created ideals of righteousness and citizenship along the mountain roads and through the trackless forests where civilisation walked with slow, yet conquering step." [1] They had their reward in the growth of their Church. So great was their success that within a few years of entering Kentucky they had won 2500 members in that State alone. In 1808, or within forty years of its first introduction, Methodism had so increased that it numbered in America 140,000 communicants. To-day, after a century of marvellous expansion, in which, on the whole, unlike the Roman Church, it has been little aided by direct emigration of Methodists there are

[1] Dr Faulkner in *A New History of Methodism*, ii. 99.

in the United States over 45,000 ordained ministers
of the various Methodist Churches, and more than
seven and a half millions of communicants, in addition to the millions of Sunday School scholars and
adult adherents. In most parts of the United States,
Methodism is to-day the predominant Church, with
a responsibility, therefore, for the future development of that mighty nation, which it is impossible
to exaggerate.

II

Any sketch, however slight, of the history of
Methodism in the New World, must lie beyond our
scope. But one or two special points demand our
attention. The first and most important is its
episcopal form of government. Throughout life
Wesley believed the episcopal form of government
to be scriptural and apostolical. But as early as
1756, owing to his reading Lord Chancellor King's
Primitive Church, he had retracted the opinion
" which I once heartily espoused " that it was
" prescribed in the Scripture." " Uninterrupted
succession," he added at a later date, " I know to be
a fable which no man ever did or can prove." He
had further convinced himself that, " bishops and
presbyters are of the same order, and consequently
have the same right to ordain." Holding these

views, the plight of the American societies, where for hundreds of miles together there was no one to administer the Sacraments, as also the partial wreck and complete disorganisation in America of the Anglican Church, forced him to act. On the failure of his two attempts to persuade Bishop Lowth to ordain at least one of his preachers, he wrote :—

" As our American brethren are now totally disentangled both from the State and from the English hierarchy, we dare not entangle them again either with the one or the other."

So in 1784, in conjunction with two other Anglican presbyters, he ordained two " elders " for England, and " Thomas Coke, LL.D., superintendent for the Church of God under our care in North America," with instructions on his arrival in America, to consecrate Francis Asbury to the same office. Though Wesley did not approve of the use of the title of " bishop " in these ordinations, the American Methodists at once interpreted the word as such— as indeed, Charles Wesley had done already. The outcome was the organisation in America, on the arrival of Coke, of the Methodist Church on an episcopal basis. On this basis in all its branches, it has ever since continued. The Methodist Episcopal Church, with its 3,000,000 communicants and

19,000 ministers, has 26 bishops; the Methodist
Episcopal Church South with its 1,656,000 communicants, and 7000 ministers, has 11 bishops.

In consequence, possibly, of this government by
an episcopacy, combined with the national character, the Methodist Church of America is both
curiously conservative and yet democratic. The
power of its bishops, especially in the location of the
ministers, would scarcely be tolerated by any Church
in England; while laymen have a very subordinate
place in the councils and courts of the Methodist
Episcopal Church, compared with the rights they
possess in England, even in the conservative
Wesleyan Methodist Church. The democratic side
is seen in the comparative unimportance of the
bishops at the great quadrennial Conferences, at
which alone legislation can be passed. In the
interval between these conferences their powers as
executive officers may seem to some to be excessive;
at the conferences themselves they preside but are
not allowed to speak. With American Methodists
the episcopacy, though strongly cherished, is care-
fully guarded. In reality it is not the outcome of
any ecclesiastical theory but a great instrument
for securing effective administration.

In the development of its inner life, one feature
assumed in past days a prominence in American
Methodism out of all proportion, perhaps, to its

real importance. We allude to its famous camp-meetings. In their origin they were the result of the physical conditions of the country. The widely-scattered congregations came together at stated times, at some central place, where there was a good supply of water and other conveniences, and there spent a few days in worship and social intercourse. But with a more settled country and ministry, these camp-meetings, with their dangers and advantages, became a thing of the past.

The great difficulty of American Methodism from the first was the question of slavery. To this, and not to disputes either over doctrine or, as in the old country, over church polity, must be ascribed the divisions of Methodism in the United States. That the coloured people were organised at an early date within separate folds of their own, was perhaps inevitable ; the misfortune was that slavery led to a fatal dissension between North and South in the Methodist Episcopal Church. Into the merits of the controversy it is difficult at this time of day to enter with impartiality. Slavery is regarded by all as " the sum of all villanies " which Wesley uncompromisingly proclaimed it to be, and the early Methodist preachers of America, almost to a man, were abolitionists. But the " peculiar institution " of the South was too strong for them, and the many efforts of Conference to promote emancipation issued in 1816 in a compromise which practically followed the lines of political cleavage over the same difficult subject. The slow but inevitable breakdown of the political compromise is a matter of general history, and led to the great civil war between North and South. In the Methodist Church, where the issues were less involved than at Washington, the separation took place twenty years earlier. In 1845 the great American Episcopal Church South split off from the North. In the political world, the genius of Lincoln, and the determination of Grant, saved the unity of the commonwealth; but to this day the Methodism of North and South has continued apart. Of recent years the old bitterness has largely passed away, and there are hopeful signs that in the future, be it far or near, the Methodism of North and South, will again be one. But it is probable that the two million coloured Methodists will still remain apart, if only through the influence of their growing race consciousness.

III

In other lands of the English-speaking race Methodism has also done well, though nowhere securing the prominence that has fallen to her in the States. In Canada, Australia and New Zealand, as in the United States, she has had the opportunity of a new world in the making. In 1791, for instance, the population of Upper Canada—the modern Ontario—was not above 10,000, with not a dozen Protestant clergy along the whole St Lawrence. But as the new settlers passed into the country the " saddle-bag brigade " of Methodist preachers, followed them up. Many of these were men of but little culture, but in Nathan Bangs Canadian Methodism possessed a pioneer, whose name became well known throughout the whole continent. Canadian Methodism in its beginnings, was only a " district " of the Methodist Episcopal Church, but as a result of the disastrous war of 1812, between England and the United States, steps were taken which, though at first producing division, ultimately led to the whole being affiliated to the British Conference (1883) and organised upon the English rather than the American or Episcopal plan. Though the great growth of the work soon led to its establishment upon an independent footing, the close connection of Canadian with English Methodism was thus one of the bonds which linked Canada to the Old Country in the days before politicians had awaked to the value of the Empire. Great as has been the growth of Canadian Methodism, its history is even more remarkable for the spirit of union which it has displayed. Canadian Methodism, though not without its initial periods of dissension, is not only one from ocean to ocean, but steps have been taken to formulate, if possible, a basis for the organic union of the Presbyterian, Methodist, and Congregational churches of the Dominion into one great non-episcopal Evangelical Church.

In Australia, also, Methodist re-union has been a striking success. In spite of past divisions the Methodist Church of Australasia is now one, with 1000 ministers and over 100,000 communicants. Its history, from its first introduction into Sydney in 1812, has been the record of continental progress, in spite of the difficulties of work in a country which was, at first, regarded as a mere dumping ground for convicts, and which, afterwards, in the rush to the goldfields of Victoria, drew to it some of the roughest spirits of two continents. From Sydney pioneers carried the new enthusiasm into the convict hell of Tasmania, then over the seas to the Maoris of New Zealand. Fortunately, also, many of the diggers in the new goldfields were Cornish Methodists who brought with them the old fire. So great was the growth of the work, that in 1854, the Australasian mission was formed into a separate Conference, which has to-day the spiritual oversight of twelve per cent. of the whole population of Australia and New Zealand.

In South Africa, Methodism found the ground more

securely pre-occupied than in either America, Canada, or Australia. The dominant Church of South Africa, as all men know, is the Dutch. Hence the mission of Methodism has been, in the main, the attempt to reach those for whom the Dutch Church could not, or would not, provide. Originally introduced in 1806 by soldiers in the army which had recently seized Cape Town, it was not until ten years later that the Cape Methodists were able to secure a minister from England. On his arrival the Rev. Barnabas Shaw showed the Yorkshire spirit in preaching first to the soldiers, then afterwards to slaves, in spite of the governor's prohibition. Among the slaves and in a mission to the native races the South African Methodists found from the first, their chief opportunity. Their success among the Namaquas, and, later, among various Bantu tribes, has been so great that there are to-day in South Africa over 66,000 Methodist native communicants, with 30,000 on trial for membership. Not the least of the Methodist services for South Africa has been its ample provision of native schools, training colleges, and other educational equipment.

Among the white races in South Africa the chief centres of Methodist influence have been in English settlements or enclaves ; the old settlement established in 1820 round Grahamstown by the sending out of 4000 selected emigrants ; the colony estab-

lished in 1851 in Natal by the arrival of several
thousand English, largely Methodists from Yorkshire ; and, in recent years, in the Transvaal and in
Rhodesia. In both these countries many of the
miners were Methodists from Cornwall. The unifica-
tion under one South African Conference of all the
work, part of which at present is supported by,
and under the control of, the Wesleyan Missionary
Society in London, is only a matter of time and of
the growth of local resources. In the solution of
the problems which confront a federated South
Africa, the Methodist Church, with its great influence
among the natives, must play a leading part.

In another part of the world, Methodism has done
a good work among the slaves. Methodism was
introduced into the West Indies by a converted
planter of some position, Nathaniel Gilbert, and in
1786 when Dr Coke was sent out to organise the
work, there were already 2000 communicants in
Antigua alone. Coke reported that the spiritual
state of the island was most deplorable. In many
parishes there were no churches ; but the planters,
who were averse to any steps which might lead to
emancipation, tried to crush out the Methodists by
legislation. In some places all preaching to negroes
was forbidden under a heavy fine ; in others it was
restricted to impossible hours, outside of which even
the singing of a hymn led to imprisonment. But

in spite of the bitterness aroused against the missionaries by the growth in England of the movement for emancipation, in spite also of the illegal persecutions to which they were subjected, the work steadily prospered.   The gift of emancipation brought difficulties of its own, through the economic disturbances which followed, while the recent economic depression in the West Indies has had a disastrous effect on all the Churches.   Owing to financial embarrassments the West Indian Conference, which had been established in 1884, found itself under the necessity of surrendering its autonomy and reverted to dependence on the mother society.   In the West Indies both Methodism and the Empire are confronted with similar problems, the solution of which will require similar patient statesmanship.

IV

In its foreign missionary enterprises Methodism has been true to the well-known motto of its leader inscribed over his monument in Westminster Abbey —" The World is my parish."   In its earliest days the work both in Ireland, in the States, and in the West Indies, was essentially of a missionary character, and sufficiently absorbed all the energies of the preachers.   The first attempt of Methodism to reach the heathen proper, did not take place until

F

after the death of Wesley, and was due to the indefatigable perseverance and generosity of Dr Coke, an Anglican clergyman, ordained in 1772, who had joined himself with enthusiasm to Wesley. Though, year after year, he found himself blocked by the refusal of the East Indian Company to allow missionaries in India, Coke did not despair. In 1812, he overcame the reluctance of his more cautious brethren by offering personally £6000 of his own, to start a mission to Ceylon, the cession of which in 1802 to the English Government offered an open door. Five missionaries were designated, and set aside, Dr Coke among them. In spite of ill health the voyage was spent by the veteran in the study of the Portuguese language, under the impression that it would be of use in Ceylon. His death at sea led to the Methodists at home realising their need of undertaking the heavy responsibilities which hitherto had rested solely upon the shoulders of Dr Coke. So on October 6th, 1813, the Wesleyan Missionary Society was formally constituted at Leeds, and by 1816 missionary work had become an integral part of the organisation of every home circuit.

The same year saw the commencement of organised missions by the Methodists of America, in the attempt to reach the Wyandot Indians. At first the work met with much opposition ; the Methodists

felt that the needs of their vast country demanded all
their resources.   But in 1820, a wider outlook pre-
vailed.   The General Conference reported that—
" Methodism itself is a missionary system.   Yield
the missionary spirit and you yield the very life-
blood of the cause."   A missionary society was
accordingly organised, and work begun among " the
pagan aborigines of this continent."   A great
mission was soon carried on among the Creeks of
Alabama, the Cherokees of Georgia, the Oneidas,
Shawnees, Mohawks and other tribes of redmen.
The most astonishing story is that of the mission to
the Flatheads.   Far away in the backwoods of
Oregon the Flatheads had heard from a wandering
trapper of the white man's God, and especially of
a book which told of the Great Spirit and how to
find Him.   So four of their number were sent far
East to find it.   After a trail of over 3000 miles
through pathless prairies and over untrodden mountains, they arrived in 1832 at St Louis.   There two
of them died, and the other two set off home in
despair.   They were returning they said " blind,
to a blind people."   They had not found the " White
man's Book of Heaven."   But " their long trail
of many moons far from the setting sun " was not
in vain.   Indirectly it led to the dispatch of Methodist missionaries to Oregon ; ultimately it formed
one of the factors which gave that vast territory

to the States at the time of the dispute over the
Oregon Territory with Great Britain (1846).

The details of the growth of the missionary work
of the Methodist Churches in England, America
—where it long since became more than the evan-
gelisation of the native Indians,—Canada, Australia,
and South Africa would demand a volume to itself.
We must restrict ourselves to a brief survey of the
different parts of the missionary field in which the
missionaries are toiling.

The missions of the English Methodists, broadly
speaking, are four in number: in India, in China,
and in West and South Africa.   In India they
have concentrated upon Ceylon, Madras, Mysore and
Bengal.   In China, their chief efforts are in Canton
and the Middle Provinces.   One feature of the
work is, however, a most successful mission recently
started in Hunan, a province so long closed to all
foreigners.   In West Africa the mission to the Gold
Coast was established as far back as 1792, and, in
its own way, has attained remarkable success,
though at a great cost, especially in former days,
of the lives of the missionaries.   In South Africa
the success of the missions to the Kaffirs, Basutos,
and Hottentots, points the way in the near future
to a determined attack from the South upon Central
Africa with its great lakes and teeming populations.

The American Methodists as far back as 1832,

began a work in Liberia, a country with special claims upon them. Of recent years they have also established many mission stations in Portuguese East Africa. As might be expected in the land of the Monroe Doctrine, Methodist missionaries have carried on a determined campaign in South America. In 1835 a commencement was made in Brazil, followed later by stations in Argentina, Uruguay, Peru, Mexico, and Chile. In spite of the opposition of the Roman clergy, good work has been accomplished. Probably, the greatest success as yet, is the winning, after a long struggle, of religious freedom, largely as the result of the unwearied efforts of Methodist missionaries.

On the opening in 1844 of the Treaty ports of China, the American Methodists at once commenced to send missionaries to the Middle Kingdom. In spite of privations, persecution and martyrdom, the work has grown steadily but surely. To-day there are in connexion with American Methodists, 1100 ordained and unordained native preachers. In addition, since 1882, there has been developed a successful mission work by the Canadian Methodists in the provinces of Sz'Chuan and Kweichau, with hospitals, schools, and more than 100 missionaries. In the fearful Boxer insurrection of 1900, hundreds of the new converts showed their fidelity by facing torture and death rather than return to their former heathenism. Nor is work among the Chinese limited to China. Both in California and in the Transvaal, Methodists have followed the Celestials and tried to win them for the Cross.

Passing by the successful American missions in India, two or three special fields claim some notice. In 1907, the Methodist Churches of America and Canada united to form a Japanese native Church, the membership of which already consists of more than 11,000 converts. The example of union thus set, will certainly be imitated elsewhere when the times are ripe. In 1896, the Methodist Episcopal Church South, also, began a very successful mission work in Korea. In Europe the American Methodists have numerous stations both in Germany and Italy. For the work in Germany, which is essentially evangelical and in no sense antagonistic to the Lutheran Church, America has special advantages in the large number of Methodist Germans in its own country. Perhaps the most difficult of all American missions is that to Bulgaria. Begun in 1857, it still continues in spite of constant persecution, of the Bulgarian atrocities of 1876, and of the embarrassment of the work, whenever possible, by the authorities. Of the Australian Methodists the chief missions are in the islands of the Pacific, including stations such as Fiji and Tonga originally founded by English sacrifice. In a past generation the name of Fiji, with the story of its conversion by such heroes of the Cross as Hunt and Calvert, was a potent source of enthusiasm and generosity. To-day the Methodist Church throughout the world, and for that matter every other church, is face to face no longer with the impressionable, infantile races of mankind, but with the entrenched superstitions and hoary civilisations of the immemorial East. The easy victories of the past have given place to the less sensational and more arduous toil of the sappers. But of the issue of the fight, if only the Church of Christ is true to herself, there can be no shadow of doubt. In the winning of the East for the Cross, Methodism must play a great part. Possibly, also, on the missionfield there may come solutions of the problems of unity which at present are but dreams, or even are regarded, from the standpoint of the difficulties at home, as impossibilities.

CHAPTER IV

THE DIVISIONS AND REUNIONS OF BRITISH METHODISM

I

WITH some misgivings we have headed this chapter
The Divisions of British Methodism. By so doing
we run the risk of undue emphasis of the accidental
at the expense of the essential. For the divisions
of Methodism, large as they loom to the outside
world, are in reality the least part of its spiritual
history. For this reason we do not propose to
inflict upon the reader any long account of the
divisions of Methodism. For the Methodist such a
chapter, within the limits that we can allow, would
be valueless ; he would justly complain that it was
impossible to set out in a few lines, without caricature

or injustice, especially to the inner spiritual life of the movement, the history of divisions the roots of which, for the most part, lie rather in personal considerations than in fundamental differences either of doctrine or government. The attempt, also, so far as the outsider is concerned, would be useless. For the divisions of Methodism have not been founded upon reasons that will commend themselves without reserve at the bar of history. Too often they have been the results of misunderstanding, or of tactless administration ; above all they have been the outcome of the " settling down " process through which every great movement and institution must pass. Nor must we overlook the influence of the strong democratic wave which characterized the century after Waterloo, in producing friction in a body so conservatively organized as was Wesley's Methodism.

In defence of Methodism we might plead that the divisions which attended this " settling down " have not been more marked or numerous than those which have accompanied every other great religious awakening. The dynamic forces which underlie a great revolt are never at first static, whatever they may become in process of time. We could illustrate this position abundantly both from the history of the Early Church, of the Reformation, of the Puritan struggle or of the great upheaval in Europe that we call the French Revolution. To find fault with this tendency to cleavage that marks all volcanic or elementary outbursts may be right and good for the *a priori* philosopher, but betrays a curious ignorance of the great facts of life. History shows that all revolts and reforms tend to carry themselves in diverse directions farther or faster than the original intentions of their leaders, and are, in consequence, accompanied by divisions which it is the wearisome task of a later generation to smoothe away. When the philosopher, in consequence, proclaims that all revolts are dangerous he may be right, but the historian who deals with facts cannot be guided by his *a priori* dictum.

If, therefore, we approach the study of Methodist divisions in this spirit, the student will not be astonished at the divisions themselves, though he may regret the causes. These, in fact, lie deep-rooted in the imperfections and limitations of all human movements, however spiritual in intention. Instead, therefore, of attempting to trace in detail the schisms in British Methodism, or to narrate the history of the sections, we shall restrict ourselves to the indication of the causes which led to these divisions, with some reflections at the close upon the prospects of the healing of the same.

II

The first dissension in Methodism arose between Whitefield and Wesley over the question of Calvinism. In reality Arminianism and Calvinism are so irreconcilable that it is difficult to conceive how the two opposing theologies could ever, under any circumstances, have been combined in one body. It was fortunate that the separation occurred during Wesley's lifetime ; it was disastrous that the controversy on both sides was conducted with more than usual theological positiveness. Finally, after both sides had considerably modified their first crude dogmatism, both went their several ways. Whitefield established his own societies ; Wesley, supported by the powerful pen of Fletcher, went on to perfect his organisation. Another important result was the drifting away from Methodism of the Evangelicals, with Toplady, Berridge, Vernon and Romaine at their head. Whatever be the merits of the controversy, logically or theologically, the verdict of time has been for Wesley. Except in Wales, Calvinistic Methodism is now as extinct as Evangelical Calvinism in the Church of England. For that matter, within living memory, the doctrine of the universality of the gospel call has passed from an argument into a conviction, which, like every other fundamental conviction, is not dependent

upon proof, nor assailable because of logical difficulties. Rightly or wrongly, the average Christian
has settled the matter for himself by falling back
upon his own consciousness of the fitness of things,
of what is possible or probable in a moral world
under a moral governor. The controversy, though
all consuming in its day, is as dead as the great
struggle which rent the thirteenth century between
the Zealots or Spiritual Franciscans and the Moderates
as to the meaning of " apostolic poverty."

The next division in Methodism was the rise of
the New Connexion in 1797. This schism, stripping
it of all personal misunderstandings, was the result
of the indeterminate relationship to the Anglican
Church in which Wesley at his death had left his
societies. In 1784, by his Deed of Declaration,
Wesley, whether consciously or not, had taken the
final step of separation, by providing the machinery
for the continuation and government of his societies
upon his decease. In place of a successor he had
appointed a conference of one hundred preachers—
the Legal Hundred, as its shadow is now designated
—to take his place, with all his rights and privileges,
providing always that they maintained both the
doctrines and itinerancy of Methodism unchanged.
But Wesley, though thus constituting a separate
Church, had taken few steps to provide for the
administration of the Sacraments except by attend-

ance at the parish church. How completely he had exaggerated the attachment of both preachers and people to the Established Church, is shown in the demand which arose, immediately upon his decease, for the settlement of this question.

As usual in such cases there were two parties ; the one, cautious and conservative ; the other, anxious to carry out logic to its conclusions without hesitation or delay. Without doubt the balance inclined towards the more cautious policy. The " Church Methodists," especially in London, were in the majority, and if the Anglican bishops had been wise in their generation, there is little doubt that they could have entered into some arrangement which would have satisfied the majority and anchored Methodism as a society to the Church of England. But the opportunity passed, and the unwillingness of the clergy to allow Methodists to participate at the Lord's Table forced the question more definitely upon a reluctant Conference. The answer given was neither logical nor heroic. By the Plan of Pacification of 1795 each separate " society " was allowed to settle for itself the question of the holding of its services within " church hours," as also of the administration of the Sacraments by its preachers. This method of local option, though difficult to defend upon theological grounds, proved, on the whole, a statesmanlike solution. It satisfied

the great majority of the societies, and provided a
way, illogical, perhaps, but cautious, for future
complete separation of Methodism and Anglicanism.
In the next generation the adoption of the " Plan "
became universal.

But, naturally, there were some whom this
method of settlement of a great question did not
satisfy. They desired to force more logical conclusions upon a reluctant community. They were
unwilling to await the settlement that the great
logician, Time, would inevitably effect. This party,
under the lead of Alexander Kilham, put forth
counter proposals of their own, the general effect
of which would have been a considerable alteration
in Methodism, amounting in some details to a revolution. These proposals may be called " statesmanlike and prescient " provided we understand our
terms. They have long since been adopted in the
main by the most conservative Methodists ; judged
merely from the standpoint of to-day it is difficult
to conceive that they should ever have been opposed.
But when they were put forward they were altogether
in advance of the general demand, and their adoption
would undoubtedly have led to a greater schism than
their rejection. The party of cautious advance was
in the majority, and, as the result of unwise action
on both sides, the party of logical hurry withdrew,
founding, in 1797, The Methodist New Connexion.

The next division in Methodism was the result of the emotional " revivalism " which was so rife at the opening of the nineteenth century, especially in the North of England. Hard things may be said, ofttimes with justice, about these " revivalists," as hard things have always been said about men supremely in earnest. They pushed individualism to an extreme. Like George Fox they laid supreme stress on the inner light. They subordinated, as Wesley had done before them, Church order and regulations to soul saving and individual edification. Undoubtedly they gave too much play to the emotional as distinct from the more intellectual aspects of religion. They delighted in the camp-meetings at Mow Cop and elsewhere, which had formed so remarkable a feature in America. If Methodist officials had been wise, they might, per-haps, have controlled these extremists by giving them fair latitude as mission bands auxiliary to the regular societies, as irregular cavalry in the host of the Lord. As it was, they acted towards them with the unwisdom with which the Anglican bishops had acted towards their fathers. Wesleyan Method-ism, in fact, at this time was setting its house in order ; it was cautiously constituting its organisa-tion and complete independence. The thing it most dreaded was irregularity—always the supreme anxiety of courts that are seeking to regularise their

own affairs, especially when they are keenly conscious
of the criticism of those from whom they are seceding.
The consequence was the separation (1808-1811),
under William Clowes and Hugh Bourne, of the
Primitive Methodists as a separate organisation.

Though at first almost confined to Staffordshire
the zeal of the Primitive Methodists, the devotion
of its ministers, indifferent to persecution, ridicule
or poverty, led to its rapid growth, especially in East
Anglia. One striking feature of its work was the
extent to which women participated, both as local
preachers, and even, in early days, as travelling
preachers and missionaries. In the social life of
England Primitive Methodist local preachers have
played a great part by the leadership they have
given to the working classes. The excessive individualism which marked the birth of the movement has long since passed away, as also has the
over-abundant emotionalism. With the closing
years of the nineteenth century the Primitive
Methodists acquired a deep sense of the value both
of culture and connexionalism, and a strong determination to work out the development of their
Church on broad, comprehensive lines.

Another branch of Methodists, the Bible Christians,
arose from similar causes. The spiritual needs of
Devon and Cornwall weighed upon the soul of
William O'Bryan. When he offered himself as an

itinerant the Wesleyan Methodists of Cornwall could not see their way to accept him, inasmuch as he was a married man. Consumed with zeal, he made light of discipline. But between his own irregularities on one side and martinets on the other, the result was inevitable, and O'Bryan withdrew (1815) that he might work on his own lines. The community he formed was not so much a secession from Methodism as a fresh ingathering of the neglected. Through the length and breadth of Cornwall and Devon, the Bible Christians toiled with a passionate earnestness which made light of persecution, and that no poverty could daunt. But in the early years of the nineteenth century Cornwall and Devon were still cut off from the rest of England, and the community that O'Bryan formed thus remained strictly local.

We believe that, on the whole, both Primitive Methodists and Bible Christians have accomplished more by separate existence than they would have done otherwise. They have not so much weakened Methodism as gathered in classes that might otherwise never have been reached, or which would not have been contented with the less democratic government of the original societies. But, as little can be said in defence of the causes which led to the schism of the New Connexion, so still less can be said in defence of the great disruption of 1849,

G

the issue of which was the rise of the United Methodists. For Wesleyan Methodists the first fifty years of the century had been years of astonishing growth. In every part of the country they had built stately chapels, oftentimes crowded with large congregations. Their class-meetings, band meetings, prayer-meetings, were full of vigour and spiritual life. At the same time there had been a wonderful development in organisation. Under the leadership of four men of remarkable power—Jabez Bunting, Adam Clark, Richard Watson, and Robert Newton— the inchoate society which John Wesley had left had become a powerful, compact Church, conscious of its independence, determined to fulfil all its legitimate functions.

Of the four leaders to whom we have referred, Newton was famous for his gifts as an orator, Watson for his powers as a preacher and writer, especially in theology, and Adam Clark for his scholarship. But the greatest of the four undoubtedly was Bunting. For over forty years he was the acknowledged ruler of Methodism. So far from being, as is often supposed, intolerant of change, to Bunting must be attributed the initiative in the measures which have secured for the Methodist laity legislative and administrative privileges of which Wesley had never dreamed. But like many other statesmen of the first order he was too masterful ; he neither allowed his opponents free play, nor was he as careful as he should have been to disassociate himself from some unworthy syco- phants. In his later years also, he seems scarcely to have realised the need of the further develop- ment, with the changing times, of the principles which he had been the first adequately to expound. The consequence was the rise of a spirit of dis- affection, which found its issue, through the bitter pen of James Everett, in the publication of anony- mous *Fly Sheets* (1846-8). The unworthy character of these squibs cannot be defended ; nor, unfortun- ately, can much be said for the methods that were taken in the Wesleyan Conference to discover and punish the authors.

The result was a schism which reflected credit on nobody, the details of which are better for- gotten. But the effects cannot be so easily dis- missed. Over 100,000 communicants withdrew to form a separate organisation, afterwards known as United Methodists. Nor was this numerical loss the worst part. In some places Methodism, by being rent asunder, was almost destroyed, and has never recovered from the wounds inflicted by the foes of its own household. In others, those who had withdrawn, though sometimes politically noisy, were often the most ardent and spiritually fervent. Through the retirement of these forwards too often

a dismal lethargy took possession of those who
remained, the effects of which were felt long afterwards. Even where there was no lethargy, for
years the energies which should have been employed
in aggression were used up in the effort to support
the existing crippled agencies. Politically also,
the results were disastrous. The withdrawal of the
liberal section led to the identification of Wesleyan
Methodism too closely with the conservative party,
with a natural reaction, or tendency to reaction, in
later years that has had equal dangers and dis-
advantages. Only one good thing came out of the
deplorable controversy. The Wesleyan Conference
learned its lesson ; the history of its proceedings for
half a century has been one of steady development
of the privileges and responsibilities of the laity,
while at the same time duly conserving the
pastoral functions. The invaluable work in these
matters, both of Dr Rigg and of Hugh Price Hughes,
can never be forgotten. To Hughes, also, it was
given to arouse once more under new forms the old
enthusiasms, and, in his own impetuous way, to
point to broader ideals of service and influence.
If Methodism had been organised in 1797 or 1849
as it is organised in 1912, no schism or division
would ever have arisen. But, on the other hand,
possibly such wise and liberal organisation and
temper would never have arisen had Methodism

not learned through disaster and schism the advantages of a far-sighted comprehensiveness. Through the friction of past days, Methodism in all its branches has learned the value of a government based upon a conservative yet democratic basis, in which shall be conserved the essentials of stability and progress.

III

That Methodism has now got over the " sturm und drang " of its youth, that the process of " settling down " has now virtually been completed, will be admitted by most intelligent observers. The days of individualism and schism, the spirit of sect which seems to be a necessary force in some stages of religious growth, have now given place to a deeper conception of solidarity ; the tendency to-day is all towards reunion rather than further division. But, as the history of the Church has always shown, divisions are not so easily rectified as created, even when, as in the case of Methodism, there are absolutely no theological differences to overcome. There are vested interests of all sorts, not necessarily material, which are not easily accommodated, though the animosities originally engendered have passed away.

Something, no doubt, has been accomplished already in Methodism towards reunion. In Ireland,

in Australia, and in Canada, the Methodist Church
to-day is one. To the deeper divisions in the United
States and the chances of unity we have already
referred.[1] Even in the Old Country the last
quarter of a century has seen a wonderful development of amity. On all hands the evils and weakness
of division are recognised ; there is no longer the
burning desire to build four different Methodist
chapels in a village that could scarcely support one.
But to undo the past is not easy of accomplishment.
Mere legislation, or even the convictions of the
ministers and more intelligent laity, would accomplish nothing except cause further division unless
they carried with them the practical unanimity of
all classes. That, in the providence of God, this will
come can scarcely be doubted. But the time is
not yet. Much spade work has yet to be done
before the foundations of a united Methodism can
be securely laid. There are financial obstacles to
be overcome ; difficulties with reference to the
different status and equipment of the ministry ;
and also—in spite of the growing liberalism of the
original Methodism, and the growing conservatism
of the seceders—a few, not many, difficulties of
constitution and organisation. Above all there
is the supreme need of a great sweep through the
length and breadth of the land of the influence of

[1] *Supra*, p. 76.

the Holy Spirit. When this comes faith will laugh
at impossibilities, and love rejoice to dwell on the
deeper things wherein there is agreement, to the
exclusion of the more trivial differences. In the
meanwhile haste may do mischief, and mechanical
combinations prevent ultimate organic fusions.

One great reunion in England has, however, been
accomplished, which demands some notice, both
for its own sake and as an omen of the future. We
allude to the reunion, under the title of the United
Methodist Church, of the divisions alluded to in these
pages as the New Connexion, the Bible Christians,
and the United Free Methodists. After long
negotiations, which at times seemed destined to
lead to nothing, the three Conferences in 1905
adopted a basis of union. On this being referred
to the several quarterly meetings—the local courts
of the circuits of Methodism—it was adopted with
but four adverse votes. As a result of this remarkable vote the three Conferences were enabled to
obtain the necessary Act of Parliament in 1907,
and to meet in one united Conference on September
17th, 1907. This memorable reunion gained
emphasis from the fact that it was held by invita-
tion in Wesley's Chapel, City Road, the metropolitan
church of world-wide Methodism. For various
reasons the Primitive Methodists could not at the
time see their way to join in this reunion ; but it is

certainly no little advantage that but three divisions now remain. In due time, possibly within the course of another generation, the three will be still further reduced, thus paving the way for the eventual outcome when, as we believe, the Protestant religious life of England will be organically grouped under three forms—the Anglican, the Methodist, and the united Congregational and Baptist. These three forms, again, may be, we trust will be, virtually one in life and loyalty, as also in the essentials of creed, differing chiefly in methods of government.

To some of our readers such a consummation may appear meagre and inadequate. They can be satisfied with nothing short of absolute reunion—" that they all may be one." What the future may bring forth, under the guidance of the Holy Spirit, we cannot say. The questions which seem so insuperable, when viewed from a local centre, may some day be solved in ways of which at present we little dream ; as, for instance, by the great spiritual awakening of India or China, and the imperative unity which such an awakening might produce. But leaving out of account this great though not impossible contingency, if by reunion is intended the absorption of Methodism in Anglicanism, we must frankly confess that of this we see no possibility, not even in England, certainly not in the United States. Those who urge such absorption

cannot have realised that Methodism is the largest
Protestant Church in the world.   In America, from
the relative insignificance of Anglicanism, especially
in the Central and Western States, the proposition
would be laughed out of court.   But even if the
question is restricted to this country alone the
issue cannot be in doubt.   Between the Methodist
doctrine of the ministry and of the Sacraments,
and the High Anglican theory as often enunciated,
there is a gulf fixed which it were absurd to
ignore.   The virtual suppression of Evangelicalism
as a governing force in the Church of England
has made Methodism more conscious of itself as the
representative Evangelical Church of the country.
Even Wesleyan Methodism, which at one time almost
regarded itself as a sort of poor dependent of the
Established Church, has in these later years drifted
into complete separation, largely as the result of the
pressure from without of an intolerant form of
Anglicanism.   Harmony can never be restored on
the old basis.   Only the frankest recognition by
the Anglican of the validity and reality of the church
life of Methodism, including the orders of its ministers,
only the unswerving fidelity of Anglicanism to the
great principles which underlay the Reformation, can
prevent a further widening of the breach, than
which we can conceive no greater disaster of English
religious life.   Whether such recognition and

fidelity might not lead to schism in the Anglican Church itself is, however, more than doubtful, at any rate under present conditions. As things now are, a large party in the Church of England seems more anxious to secure the approval and friendship of the alien adherents of the Eastern and Roman faiths than to take steps for the consolidation of the Protestantism of the Empire. Such an outlook is, we hold, as disastrous imperially, as it is unjust to the teaching of history.

CHAPTER V

THE THEOLOGY AND POLITY OF METHODISM

I

In the present chapter we propose to give, though
in merest outline, some presentation of the doctrines
and polity of the Methodist Church, so far as these
differ in any considerable degree from the creeds
and polities of other churches. Methodist teaching
throughout the world is one, though the differences
in Methodist polity and organisation are considerable.
But, after all, true unity is determined by oneness
of creed.

The student of Methodism[1] must not expect to
find within it the enunciation of a new creed or

---

[1] The term "Methodist" was not, of course, new. Not to mention
older application of the word to students of certain schools of botany
and of medicine (on which see Murray's *New Eng. Dict.*, s.v. 1), it was
definitely applied to a class of religious people in a sermon at Lambeth
in 1647 by Farindon (*Serm.* xx. [1672] i. 394), and not as if it were
newly coined for the occasion. In 1658 J. Spencer, in *Things New and
Old*, p. 161, writes: "Where are now our Anabaptists and plain
pack-staff Methodists, who esteem all flowers of rhetoric in sermons no
better than stinking weeds, and all elegance of speech no better than
profane spells?" In 1693 a pamphlet was published entitled *A War
among the Angels of the Churches: wherein is shewed the Principles of
the New Methodists in the great point of Justification*, by a Country
Professor of Jesus Christ; see R. Traill's *Sel. Works* (1845), p. 167.
In a dictionary published by Phillips (ed. Kersey) in 1706 the word
"Methodist" is thus explained: "One that treats of method or
affects to be methodical." The application of the title to the Wesley
movement would thus seem to be a loose combination of several ideas,
and was possibly influenced by current slang to which we have now
lost the key. While undoubtedly the main emphasis would be on the
"methodical" character of the new movement, we must bear in mind
certain theological significations which may have influenced the wits
of Oxford (*cf.* C. Mather's *Magn. Chr.* (1702), iv. 132, "Parum aut
nihil asserunt Amyraldistae quos Novatores et Methodistas vocant"
(quoted in Murray, s.v.), just as the wits of Antioch were influenced
in giving the Graeco-Latin names of "Chrestians" or "Christianoi"
(see my *Persecution in the Early Church*, p. 58 n.), the latter of
which finally became used.

"Methodists" was not the first name that was given to Charles
Wesley and his friends. The nickname "Sacramentarians," which
originated in Merton College, seems to have preceded it. Many other
designations, *e.g.* Bible Moths, Holy Club, Supererogation Men, were
applied to them, but the term "Methodists" was the name that sur-

symbol of faith. Methodism, it is true, was born in a university, but in reality owed nothing to Oxford, and was soon driven out of it. Apart from this, its genius did not lie in the schools of the theologian. Like St Francis, John Wesley, the St Francis of the eighteenth century, did not set out to discover buried truth, but to live out a forgotten life, and to group together into societies those of like mind with himself. Unlike Wyclif, his object was not to overthrow existing dogmas, but to galvanise them into life. Luther was driven into a life-long fight with a great organisation ; Calvin into the working out of a creed that could take the place of the discredited absolutism of Rome. Wesley, on the contrary, was supremely anxious to serve the Church of his fathers, whose creed, as he interpreted it, appealed to him as the final word of God. To theological thought his contribution is thus insignificant and cannot for a moment be compared with the masterpieces of such leaders of revolt as Wyclif, Melancthon or Calvin ; as the apostle of primitive Christianity he has obtained an abiding place in history side by side with the heroes of the early Church. To the lead thus given by

vived. John Wesley's definition of the word in his dictionary (published in 1753) would account for the survival : "A Methodist is one who lives according to the method laid down in the Bible." The word, in accordance with the usual evolution of such terms, has reference now to the organised body of " Methodists " and not to "method."

Wesley, Methodism, on the whole, has been con-
sistent. Its genius is practical rather than theological ; for its small contribution to thought
abundant atonement has been made by its larger
contribution to life.

In the great fundamentals of the faith, the
doctrines of the Trinity, of the Incarnation, of the
Atonement, Methodism is naturally one with its
mother-church. In these essentials it is Catholic
in the true sense of that misused word.[1] It accepts
the primary historic symbols, the early Roman
symbol or Apostles' Creed, and the enlarged edition
of the Baptismal Creed of Jerusalem that passes
under the name of Nicea ; as well as the great song-
creed that we call the *Te-Deum*. From these symbols
its only difference would be some hesitation as to
the value of the late addition, " He descended into
hell," and its interpretation of the obscure clause
" sanctorum communionem," with a reference mainly
to present Christian fellowship, a meaning, we
frankly own, probably not in accord with the original
intention. To the so-called Athanasian Creed, in
reality a symbol of Gallic, possibly Spanish, origin,

---

[1] For a fuller exposition of the doctrines of Methodism in their
relation to the development of the Christian Church and in their
reference to religious psychology I may perhaps refer to my chapter
in *A New History of Methodism*, vol. i. c. 1.   " The Place of
Methodism in the Christian Church."

designed as a condemnation of Apollinarian doctrine, Methodism attaches little practical value, at any rate in its present form, inasmuch as its logical subtleties savour rather of the schools than of life. But in this rejection of this great song—for so it should properly be regarded—as the shibboleth of faith, Methodism is one with the Eastern Church.

In its doctrine of the Atonement, Methodism is Arminian and Evangelical. The Arminianism of Wesley, historically considered, was a legacy of Archbishop Laud, who, as part of his protest against Geneva, laid stress upon the universal aspect of the life and faith of the Church. Through the Wesleys this part of Laud's high-churchmanship has passed into the life-blood of Methodism. To the twentieth century Arminianism seems almost axiomatic, largely, of course, because the century starts with the postulate of the Fatherhood of God. The Calvinism that appealed so powerfully to the eighteenth century is to-day a discredited faith. The universality of the gospel-call is now the belief of most men. That this is so must be attributed largely to the influence of Methodist teaching ; though the all pervasive universalism of the age, avowedly based upon what is possible or probable in a moral world under a moral governor, should not be ignored. The Methodist doctrine of the Atonement is also Evangelical. It proclaims that religion is the individual consciousness of relation to God, and that this relationship is the result of personal appropriation of, or trust in, Jesus Christ and not the outcome of organisation or the gift of any priesthood. With this fundamental truth she will allow no tampering. Upon this consciousness she lays the utmost stress. This consciousness has given to its preaching its greatest power, is the explanation of its fervid evangelistic appeals, and lies at the root of its special institution of the class-meeting. For Methodism to cease from the proclamation of this doctrine would be to deny the grounds of her existence.

This personal consciousness of relationship to God through Jesus Christ is technically known as the doctrine of Assurance. In the eighteenth century Wesley's formulation of Assurance was looked upon as a dangerous innovation. One Methodist preacher was actually imprisoned for saying that he knew that his sins were forgiven. At first, also, Wesley preached the doctrine in an extreme and uncharitable form, nor did he always remember how long he himself had taken to learn its truth. But putting on one side the exaggerations of the doctrine, and the dangers into which such exaggerations lead, we can see that the doctrine of Assurance is in reality the appeal to experience. This is the fundamental contribution of Methodism to the life and thought of the Church. And as such it is wonderfully congruent with the best scientific and philosophic thought of to-day.   If we have read aright the drift of thought in the last thirty years, it has set in steadily towards the recognition of the reality of the phenomena of experience.   And chiefest of these phenomena is the religious consciousness, the validity of which cannot be questioned without questioning the grounds of being.   Tolstoy is not now alone in his claim that faith is among the forces by which men live, " without which I myself would not exist."   Such faith, according to Methodist teaching, is not only personal but conscious of the attainment of its object.

A corollary of the stress thus laid by Methodism upon religion as the personal consciousness of relationship to God is the Methodist doctrine of conversion.   As religious life itself is a consciousness, so also is conversion.   Now, as a rule, this consciousness has its beginning in time, though a deeper analysis would show that this is not invariable ; nor for that matter is " time " the vulgar equivalent for the ticks of the pendulum.   Time is not an actuality so much as a quality of consciousness. In the past, we must allow, Methodism often laid unwise stress upon the time-factor, and also made the common mistake of interpreting a vivid or full consciousness as " instantaneousness " ; though in reality the two things belong to different planes of

H

thought. But this stress upon time is, after all, a detail, to the dangers of whose exaggeration Methodists to-day are fully alive. But on the fact of conversion, *i.e.* the fact of a present conscious life in Christ, Methodism is no less careful to insist than in the past.

The same criticism and defence may be made as regards the Methodist doctrine of Holiness or " perfect love." Wesley's doctrine is really a corollary of his appeal to experience. For if a son is conscious of his relation to his Father there must be the possibility that that consciousness shall be complete, and as such the source of exquisite joy and untroubled confidence. That this is possible now is a further necessity, for otherwise the experience would not be in consciousness. But when we begin to give the full content of this consciousness, to subject it to analysis, to write down cause and effect, to express it in theological terms, then difficulties begin, and from these difficulties Wesley's statements are by no means exempt. In reality, with Wesley, holiness is not a theory but an experience, a life. But this is true of the saints of God in all generations. The wise theologian will insist on the fact, nor will he be anxious to insist on applying to this grace the categories of time and cause. In every age the desire for holiness has been the mark of the child of God. Varieties in the definition of the mark are immaterial : it is the conscious pursuit that gives unity to the lives of the saints of all time. If we must dwell upon differences we would point out that in the main, they are found in the laying of the stress either upon probation—as with the medieval saints—or upon grace—as with Wesley and St Augustine. From these two great differences spring the differences in the method of pursuit, though, after all, the end is the same, and, in the long run, it is the end that is all important.

The defects of one generation are not easily remedied by the clearer discernment of a later age. The inability of the eighteenth century to understand the life and religion of a child, reference to which has been already made,[1] unfortunately led to Methodism making no proper provision either for the oversight of its baptised children, or for the recognition by the Church of its children, when they came to years of discretion. The lack of something in Methodism corresponding—of course, with the necessary alterations which the Methodist position involves—to the Anglican Confirmation service has often been deplored, by none more than by a growing number of Methodists themselves. The fact that Wesley, with all his Anglican training, failed to make such provision, must be attributed either to his unwillingness to recognise that the Confirmation-Service of the Anglican Church was no longer avail-

[1] *Supra*, p. 55.

able, even if desired, for his adherents, or else to the general inability to understand child-religion. For long years after his death a rigid and narrow theory of conversion, suitable possibly for many adults, unsuited for the child of pious parents, prevented the Methodist people from realising the need of making proper provision for public confession of faith by those who had never left the Father's house for the Far Country. Nor were they fully aware of the loss involved by the want of a formal reception of the adolescent into the Church of Christ. Though in recent years, many attempts have been made, both by guilds, junior classes, and other organisations to solve the difficulty, it cannot be said that Methodism has yet found the bridge that she needs between the Sunday School, the home, and the Church. In consequence she has sometimes been charged, not always unjustly, with showing greater powers of conversion than of conservation.

Hard words have sometimes been said as to the theology of Methodism, that it is narrow, illiberal, and one-sided. But the life and thought of a Church is always larger and deeper than its official documents. We should pity the student who should try to understand the genius of the Church of England by a diligent consideration of its Thirty-nine Articles. So also with Methodism. In its origins Methodism stood for the insistence upon

certain doctrines that seemed to be fundamental—
the depravity of human nature, the need of conscious faith and definite conversion, the necessity
of sanctification after justification, the witness of
the Spirit, and so on. Some of these, no doubt,
were expressed in language that is now out of date,
and drawn out from a standpoint that to the
twentieth century seems unintelligible. Exactly
the same thing might be said of Nicea and of the
teaching of St Augustine. The twentieth century
may not approve of the fourth-century metaphysics,
may be bewildered by terms some of which have lost
their meaning, or may dismiss as hopelessly contra-
dictory the positions of St Augustine. Nevertheless
the creeds remain because there was in them the
dynamic of a living faith. They have lived because
they are among the affirmatives and imperatives
which from time to time, surge up in consciousness,
and which carry a larger authority than belongs to
any dialectics. They have survived the wear and
tear of centuries, because in a real way, they embodied vital experience. No student would ever
maintain that the creeds embody the whole of
theology ; they single out those features which
formed the battlefield of the moment. They
are the monuments more lasting than brass, erected
to the triumph of certain vital positions. Similar
remarks might be made as to St Augustine. So

also with the primary documents and doctrines of Methodism. The facts of experience to which they point, must not be judged by the language and arguments which Wesley and Fletcher used in their support. Metaphysics, methods of reasoning, above all methods of scriptural interpretation, change with the changing ages—the facts of the soul alone are constant. Methodism to-day, though seeking to express itself in more modern language, and from the standpoint of a wider and more liberal interpretation of the Scriptures,[1] sees no reason to believe that the experiences of the heart to which she appeals, are fundamentally different from what they were in the days of her origin.

With more justification the critic might urge that Methodism is one-sided, that she lays too much stress on certain doctrines to the neglect of others, that while clear and distinct in her teaching as to conversion and holiness, she is uncertain in her emphasis of the Sacraments, and nebulous in her notion of the Church. Such a charge seems to us exaggerated. If true—and we are not concerned to deny a measure of truth,—it was true rather of the past than of the present, and will be less true of the future than of

[1] Fortunately Methodism in its official documents is not hampered by any theory of inspiration; it insists merely on the fact without any dogma as to the method or limits. Its appeal to experience as one test of the spiritually true is, in fact, not far removed from the standpoint of sound critical methods of Biblical interpretation.

to-day.   After all it is not much more than a hundred
years since the death of Wesley, and in the life of a
Church that is but a span.   Methodism to-day
is paying increasing attention to the teaching of the
full truth as it is in Christ, including the need of
the Sacraments, the objective grace involved therein,
and the meaning and claims of the Church.   From
the experience of the individual she is turning to the
experience of the body corporate.   To the validity
of this experience, to the laws of its growth and
development she is now giving more careful consideration.   The individualism of the eighteenth
century has yielded to the modern conceptions of
solidarity.

II

We have left but scanty room for a brief description of the polity of Methodism.   Methodism, undoubtedly is Presbyterian in the main outlines of
its organisation, both in England and America.
The Presbyterian stamp was impressed upon it,
curious as it may seem, by Wesley himself, unconsciously, no doubt, for the most part.   But
Wesley's " superintendents," or elder-minister in
each " circuit " or parish, his system of " stewards "
and " leaders," his annual " conferences," his
" quarterly meetings " of the ministers and laymen

in every circuit, all fell in so closely with the Presbyterian system that the later division into synods, the later ordination of the ministers by the laying on of hands of the senior brethren, the emphasis and value placed upon the pastoral office, the later admission of the laity to all the courts of the Church, have consolidated not altered the work he began.

For the outsider some explanation may, perhaps, be necessary of these different terms and courts. The germ-cell of Methodism, as every one knows, is the class-meeting.[1] Wherever there is a class-meeting there is a Methodist society ; in Methodism a church without a class-meeting is almost inconceivable, at any rate it was inconceivable until very recently. At one time the class-meeting was of a somewhat rigid character, and personal testimony or experience was almost enforced. In these days personal testimony is, perhaps, the exception ; but the open fellowship of believers in prayer, meditation, and praise is of none the less value both for building up the Church and for the maintenance of the more public worship. Over every class, the numbers in which vary, there is a leader, generally a layman, who, though not ordained for this office is yet solemnly and deliberately chosen. Each

[1] In the following sections I have disregarded sectional differences. The description is only strictly accurate of English Wesleyan Methodists,

leader is held responsible for the oversight of the members of his class, and for reporting to the minister cases of sickness, of indifference, and the like, while regular meetings of the ministers and leaders give full opportunity for systematic oversight of the whole society and church.   It will be evident that where the system is properly worked, it is most efficient both for obtaining its immediate purpose, and for using to the full the services of the godly laity, men and women.   In country districts especially, remote perhaps from a minister, the leaders of Methodism have nobly discharged the duties of a sub-pastorate.

Round this primary germ-cell of the class-meeting there has slowly gathered and grown up, in differing complexity according to local circumstances, all the equipment of a modern church—Sunday schools, guilds, and the rest.   But on these, as they are in nowise peculiar to Methodism, it is not necessary to linger.

Methodism differs from Congregationalism in that it does not allow the society or societies in any one place to form a separate Church.   All the societies within a given area, the size of which will depend upon population and other circumstances, are grouped together into a " circuit " with two or more ministers attached to it.   The senior of such ministers is called the " superintendent " and is held

responsible for the due discharge of the duties both
of himself and of those appointed to work under
him.   A circuit—the name takes us back to the old
days of wide travel upon horseback, when Methodists were few and distances great—is thus a collec-
tion of societies, generally grouped round some
strong central society which is therefore expected to
give of its strength and resources to the help of the
others.   Every circuit is governed by a "quarterly
meeting" of the ministers and officers of the various
societies, and its interests are the special concern
of two lay officers, "circuit stewards," who among
other responsible duties are charged with the making
of due provision for the support of the ministers.   To
the Quarterly Meetings is given the right of inviting
their ministers, subject to the consent of Conference.
Every candidate for the ministry must also obtain
the endorsement of the Quarterly Meeting of his own
circuit, *i.e.* of those who will be the best fitted to
know his character and general promise.   But
important as are the rights of Quarterly Meetings,
they are not, as a rule, allowed any voice in the
pastoral matters of the Church, the admission of
members, the exercise of discipline, or the selection
of lay preachers.   These are left to the ministers
acting in consultation with the leaders of the classes.
Thus, in some respects, the courts of the germ-cell
or societies, are kept distinct from the courts of the

Church that has grown round them with its more diverse interests.

Before we pass away from the society a word should be said upon the " local preachers " of Methodism. " Local preachers " are laymen who while pursuing their daily business, yet render assistance on Sunday in preaching; generally in the smaller country chapels. Before a layman can become a local preacher he is subjected to trial and examination, especially as regards his preaching ability. As regards this last Methodists are exacting, though the standard in other respects might be raised with advantage. Without its noble army of local preachers Methodism, with its thousands of chapels too small or too poor to provide a resident minister, would be in a parlous condition, and would rapidly become a matter of the towns only. The circulation of the local preachers within a circuit, Sunday by Sunday, also serves to bind together the interests of the diverse places ; the weakest, smallest chapel becomes an object of interest and prayer for the succession of laymen who visit it. In its " local preachers " and " leaders " Methodism has made that effective use of its laity, without which every Church is shorn of its greatest strength.

The connexionalism of Methodism is further seen in the grouping of the various circuits into a number of " Districts "—the Anglican equivalent

would be dioceses. At the head of each " district "
is a " chairman " with certain well-defined though
limited powers of interfering, when necessary, with
the superintendents and circuits of his district.
All the ministers and circuit-stewards of every
district also meet twice a year, under the super-
intendence of the " chairman," for the discussion
and discharge of the work of the district, the supervision of missions, of funds, in a word of all matters
common to the various circuits.

From the society, the circuit, the district, we pass
by a natural evolution to the Conference—remember-
ing always that as a matter of fact, Wesley began his
Conferences or annual assemblies of his friends and
itinerant helpers before either circuit or district was
evolved. In Methodism, the Conference which meets
annually under a presiding officer or " President " [1]
is the supreme court of appeal, and the final executive,
thus giving to Methodism its pre-eminent " connexionalism." In all branches of Methodism the
Conference consists of ministers and laymen in

[1] The President of the Wesleyan Methodist Conference is annually
chosen by a silent ballot of the ministers without nomination or
speeches—a method of election that is, we believe, without parallel
save for the papal chair. He must, of course, be a minister.
Theoretically he is " President " only of the Conference, and with
the Conference his powers originally lapsed. But practice has long
since outgrown the restrictions imposed by early jealousy of any
successor to Wesley's autocracy.

varying proportions ; but as a rule the purely
pastoral matters of the Church—the acceptance and
ordination of candidates, doctrinal or disciplinary
lapses of the ministry, and the like—are left to the
ministers sitting apart.   To be elected to Conference
by his district Synod or by the Conference itself
is looked upon as the supreme honour of a Methodist
layman's life.

We must not pass from the Conference without
drawing attention to a curious fact.   The Conference,
as originally founded by Wesley in his famous deed-
poll, is a statutory body of one hundred ministers
elected for life.   To this " Legal Hundred " Wesley
entrusted all the rights and duties that he had
acquired or exercised, whether as regards property
or the internal affairs of the Connexion.   As
regards property the years that have elapsed since
Wesley's death has only strengthened the hold of
the Conference ;   nearly all the properties of
Methodism are now securely held on identical
trusts—" model deeds " as they are called—for the
use of the Conference.   But the Conference itself
has suffered a marvellous " sea change " that would
have astonished no one more than Wesley himself.
The ministerial Legal Hundred is still maintained
by a legal fiction as the sole Conference—we allude,
of course, to the mother-Church of Methodism—
but by long established usage is expected to ratify

without discussion or question, all the acts and discussions of the large representative gathering of ministers and laymen, in which, for all practical purposes, it is now wholly merged.[1] To be elected into the " Legal Hundred " or actual legal Conference has now become a mere honour, the greatest save the presidency which his brethren can confer upon any minister. By the ingenious use of legal forms all the advantages of the existence of a small statutory body are thus retained, together with the utmost freedom in its own internal organisation.

Two things, however, the Wesleyan Methodist Conference—the heir of Wesley's deed-poll or legal act of enrolment—cannot do. It cannot alter the doctrinal standards of Methodism, nor can it do away with the " itinerancy " of the ministers ; that system which seems so strange to outsiders, whereby every few years, ministers must leave their circuits and seek " fresh woods and pastures new." In spite of various means for mitigating the rigours of this enforced itinerancy, in Wesleyan Methodism the location of ministers in fixed charges, much as it is desired in many quarters, especially in the towns,

[1] This ratification takes place at the close of the Conference. The minutes of the Conference are rapidly read over and then adopted as the acts and resolutions of the Legal Hundred. If any point must be decided before the close, e.g. an expulsion of a minister for misconduct, a separate vote of the Legal Hundred is taken at the time.

is impossible without an enabling act of Parliament. But as a compensation, Methodist ministers are never left without some sphere of work ; there are no " stickit ministers," no curates waiting long years for preferment ; none of the troubles that afflict congregations and pastors, while awaiting or giving " calls." All changes are made at the same time,[1] and care is taken that years of service shall have their due return.   In order the better to work the system there is a rule that the salaries of all ministers shall be reduced to much of a level ; the highest minister in the Church, the President of the Conference himself, receiving very little, if anything, more than most of his brethren. On the other hand, the financial poverty of many ministers in other Churches is not allowed, Methodism, on the whole, paying all its ministers a sufficient "living wage," without, however, much surplus or chance of saving.   For every minister, on his retirement, there is also provided a small pension, while from the days of Wesley special provision has been made for the education of the sons of the manse.

III

Our limits and not our subject compel us to a conclusion.   On looking back over this inadequate sketch of a great theme we regret that in our last

[1] The first week in September in **Wesleyan Methodism.**

word, we should seem to dwell on matters of organisation. The Methodism genius for organisation and finance is indeed remarkable, and is due to the complete co-operation in its working of devoted laymen. But no Church can live either by organisation or finance ; for the secret of Methodism we must look elsewhere. The greatness of Methodism as a world-wide church does not, and will not, lie in the millions of its adherents, nor in the magnitude and adequacy of its equipment, but in the degree to which it is true to its fundamental conviction—the personal, conscious appropriation of the Life and Passion of the Risen Christ. In the history of every Church to the thoughtful student the salient fact is not so much the human agencies as the presence of the Divine. We believe, as did the earlier Fathers : Where Jesus Christ is, there is His Church. And in the story of Methodism only. the blind and irreverent can fail to discern the presence and power of the Master. For us, as for St Ignatius :

OUR CHARTER IS JESUS CHRIST
OUR INFALLIBLE CHARTER
IS
HIS CROSS, HIS DEATH AND HIS PASSION
AND
FAITH THROUGH HIM.

SELECT BIBLIOGRAPHY [1]

A. GREAT BRITAIN IN THE EIGHTEENTH CENTURY.

ABBEY, C. J., and OVERTON, J. H. *Eng. Ch. in the 18th Cent.* (2 vols., 1896).

ASHTON, J. *Social Life at the End of the 18th Cent.* (1885).

GODLEY, A. D. *Oxford in the 18th Cent.* (1908).

LELAND, J. *View of the Principal Deistical Writers* (1807).

LECKY, W. H. *Hist. England in the 18th Cent.* (new ed., 7 vols., 1892).

—— *Hist. Ireland in the 18th Cent.* (5 vols., 1897).

OVERTON, J. H., and F. RELTON. *Ch. of England from 1714-1800* (1906).

SIMON, J. S. *The Revival of Religion in the 18th Cent.* (1907).

B. JOHN WESLEY AND THE METHODIST LEADERS.

FITCHETT, W. H. *Wesley and his Century* (1906).

JACKSON, T. *Life of C. Wesley* (1848).

—— *Lives of the Early Methodist Preachers* (6 vols., 1871).

MACDONALD, F. W. *Fletcher of Madeley* (1885).

OVERTON, J. H. *John Wesley* (1891).

RIGG, J. H. *The Living Wesley* (1891).

—— *Churchmanship of J. Wesley* (1907).

SOUTHEY, R. *Life of Wesley* (best ed., 1889).

TYERMAN, L. *Oxford Methodists* (1873).

—— *Life and Times of Wesley* (3 vols., 1890).

—— *Life of G. Whitefield* (2 vols., 1876).

WEDGEWOOD, JULIA. *J. Wesley and the Evangelical Revival of the 18th Cent.* (1870).

[1] For full Bibliography see one by present author in *New History of Methodism,* ii. pp. 533-50.

I

C. HISTORY OF LATER METHODISM.

BUCKLEY, J. W.   *Hist. of Methodists in the U.S.* (2 vols., 1896).

CROOKSHANK, C. H.   *Hist. of Methodism in Ireland* (3 vols., 1885).

KENDALL, H. B.   *Hist. of Primitive Methodists* (2 vols., 1895).

SMITH, G.   *Hist. of Wesleyan Methodism* (3 vols., 1859).

STEVENS, A.   *Hist. of Methodism* (3 vols., 1875).

—— *Hist. of Methodist Episcopal Church* (4 vols., 1864).

WORKMAN, H. B., TOWNSEND, W. J., and EAYRS, G.   *A New Hist. of Methodism* (2 vols., 1909).[1]

[1] Gives the history in all countries and divisions.

INDEX

9 781107 626584